Collins

Integrated Science 3

for the **Caribbean**

T0340536

Gene Samuel & Derek McMonagle

Advisors:

**Shameem Narine, Nadine Victor-Ayers,
Ishaq Mohammed, Sheldon Rivas & Doltan Ramsubeik**

updated

Collins

HarperCollins*Publishers* Ltd
The News Building
1 London Bridge Street
London SE1 9GF

HarperCollins*Publishers*
Macken House, 39/40 Mayor Street Upper
Dublin 1, D01 C9W8, Ireland

Updated edition 2017

10 9 8 7 6

This book is produced from independently certified FSC™ paper to ensure responsible forest management.

For more information visit: www.harpercollins.co.uk/green

ISBN 978-0-00-826304-1

Collins® is a registered trademark of HarperCollins*Publishers* Limited

www.collins.co.uk/caribbeanschools

A catalogue record for this book is available from the British Library.

Typeset by QBS Learning

Printed and bound in the UK using 100% Renewable Electricity at Martins the Printers Ltd.

Authors: Gene Samuel & Derek McMonagle
Advisors: Shameem Narine, Nadine Victor-Ayers, Ishaq Mohammed, Sheldon Rivas & Doltan Ramsubeik
Illustrators: QBS Learning
Publisher: Elaine Higgleton
Commissioning Editor: Tom Hardy
Project Management: QBS Learning
Editor: Julianna Dunn
Copy Editor: Sara Hulse
Proofreader: Aidan Gill
Cover Design: Gordon MacGilp

Gene Samuel has taught science at Forms 1 and 2 level at St. Joseph's Convent Secondary School, Castries, St Lucia and is a very experienced science teacher. She has been developing resources for use in her own school for many years.

Derek McMonagle is a leading writer of science educational materials with world-wide experience. He has developed courses at primary, secondary and advanced levels for many countries including Jamaica and the UK.

Contents

Introduction – How to use this book

Form 3

Industry

We are learning how to:

- explain the impact of human activities on the local and global environment
- appreciate the impact of industry on the environment.

This tells you what you will be learning about in this lesson.

Industry ≫

Towns and cities are not just places where people live, but also where they work. Most of the damage to the environment from urbanisation is a result of increased **industry**.

This introduces the topic.

FIG 4.8 Many of the industries that produce electricity, raw materials and the products needed by modern society also produce waste gases that pollute the atmosphere

The book has plenty of good illustrations to put the science into context.

The exhaust gases from car and truck engines also put waste gases into the air and cause **atmospheric pollution**.

Materials that are released into the environment, either accidently or deliberately, may cause severe damage to plants and animals.

FIG 4.9 An oil spillage at sea may be washed ashore and will not only kill seaweed and fish, but may also damage animals such as birds that feed on them

FIG 4.10
from a
fly or s

The populations of some sea animals, such as shrimp and red snapper, have become greatly depleted as a result of **overfishing**, together with pollution and the loss of suitable habitats. If stocks of fish fall below a certain level, it is likely that they will die out completely over time.

The effects of industry are not just felt in the urban environment. Working practices also produce problems in the countryside. Farmers use **pesticides** to protect their crops. This increases food production but at a cost to the environment.

4.4

FIG 4.11 Some insecticides are indiscriminate and will kill all insects whether they damage the crops or not

Activity 4.3

The drama of human activity

You should work in a small group for this activity. You will not need any equipment or materials but you will have to improvise by finding objects to support your role-play.

Here is what you should do:

1. Choose one of the effects industry has on the environment that were described in the lesson, or choose another you know about.
2. Write a short drama about the consequences this will have on the environment in the long-term if action is not taken now.
3. Your drama should be about three minutes long. Be prepared to act it out for the rest of the class.

Check your understanding

1. In order to conserve the environment, people must look for ways of sharing with other organisms and ways of minimising the impact of their activities on other organisms. Discuss how the provision of parks and lakes within towns might help to achieve this.

Fun fact

Water pollution is widespread in Trinidad and Tobago. Much of this is the result of industry. Industrial sources of water pollution include: wash from quarries, factory waste, overuse of chemicals such as fertilisers and pesticides, and waste oil.

Key terms

industry factories and other places where goods are processed or produced

atmospheric pollution pollution of the atmosphere by waste gases produced by industry and vehicles

overfishing removing more fish from the sea than can be replaced by natural breeding

pesticides chemicals used to control pests such as insects on crops

49

There are often some fascinating fun facts or challenge facts.

Each spread offers questions to help you to check whether you have understood the topic.

Key terms are defined on the pages where they are used.

Review of Environmental impact of human activities

- Human activity has an impact on the environment. As the population of the world increases, the effect humans have on the environment increases.
- Urbanisation is the increase in the proportion of people in a country who live in towns and cities. Urbanisation is increasing in many countries as people come to towns looking for work or for other reasons. As towns and cities grow larger, so does their impact on the environment.
- As a country develops, its industry grows larger. Industry has an impact on the environment due to increased use of land for buildings and roads, and the creation of various types of pollution.
- Genetically modified (GM) crops are food crops that have been modified by adding favourable genes. This might:
  - increase the yield
  - reduce the time until the crop is ready to harvest
  - make the crop resistant to attack by insects
  - make the crop resistant to drought.
- GM crops appear to be the answer to world food shortages but some scientists believe that they may cause damage to the environment in different ways.
- Invasive alien species (IAS) are species of organism that have been transferred from one area of the world to another, either accidentally or deliberately. Where an organism has an abundance of food and no natural enemies, its population rapidly increases at the expense of native species. IAS may also carry diseases that can be transferred to native organisms. Examples of IAS in Trinidad and Tobago include the pink mealy bug, the black wattle acacia tree, the red palm mite, the Asian green mussel and the coconut moth.
- Nature reserves are areas where human activity is strictly controlled. This allows the organisms that are found there to live in the absence of human activities, which increases their chances of flourishing. Reserves also provide a haven where people can observe and study wildlife. There are a number of nature reserves in Trinidad and Tobago.
- Deforestation is the removal of trees so that land can be used for building or for farming. The removal of trees destroys many different habitats, both in the trees and on the ground beneath them. The results of deforestation are the loss of many species of organism from an area and an increase in soil erosion.
- Biodiversity is the number of different species of organism found in an area. Biodiversity is high when an area has many different habitats. Trinidad and Tobago has the highest level of biodiversity in the whole of the Caribbean.
- Urbanisation, industry and deforestation all reduce the level of biodiversity in an area. Other human activities, such as changes in land usage, also impact on biodiversity.

At the end of each group of Units there are pages which list the key topics covered in the Units. These will be useful for revision.

Review questions on Environmental impact of human activities

1. **a)** What is meant by the term 'biodegradable'?
   b) Give three examples of materials that are:
   i) biodegradable
   ii) non-biodegradable.
   c) Why is non-biodegradable waste a threat to the environment?
2. Copy and complete the following sentences.
   a) Biodiversity is a measure of the number of different types of _____ and _____.
   b) Matura National Park is in the _____ of Trinidad.
   c) In a national park human activities are _____.
   d) In a national park the level of _____ is high because organisms are protected.
   e) One of the rare _____ living in the Matura National Park is the ocelot.
3. Copy and complete the following sentences using words from the box.

endangered	extinct	habitats	protected

   a) When land is cleared for farms natural _____ are destroyed.
   b) When populations of plants and animals fall they are said to be _____.
   c) If something is not done to conserve plants and animals they may become _____.
   d) In national parks, plants and animals are _____ from the activities of people.
4. Describe ways in which building and operating a sugar factory might harm the local environment.
5. The pawi is a bird that lives in the canopy of hill forests in Trinidad and Tobago. It feeds on fruit from the trees and builds its nest high up in them.
   a) The pawi is classified as an environmentally sensitive species in Trinidad and Tobago. What do you think this means?
   b) Suggest some reasons why any loss of forest would be detrimental to the population of pawi.
6. Scientists have developed a genetically modified corn that produces a poison that kills harmful insects. Decide whether each of the following is an advantage or a disadvantage of growing this crop.
   a) The farmer no longer has to buy insecticides.

At the end of each section there are special questions to help you and your teacher review your knowledge, and see if you can apply this knowledge and the science skills that you have developed.

Improving your local environment

Are there things about your local environment you think somebody should do something about? Maybe that somebody is you?

People are often appalled by rubbish dumped in their community but they don't know what to do about it. As a scientist you have analytical skills that can help your community.

Rubbish doesn't appear on our streets by magic. It appears because people are careless or sometimes just lazy. You are going to do what you can to improve the situation in your community.

FIG 4.62 Litter is unsightly and dangerous

1. You are going to work in a group of 3 or 4 to reduce rubbish in your community. It would be best if all of the students in your group live near one another. The tasks are:
   - to identify the areas of your community which are affected by rubbish
   - to analyse the rubbish to see what you are dealing with
   - to try and identify sources of this rubbish
   - to find out what help is available from local authorities
   - to take steps to reduce or even eliminate the rubbish on the streets of your community.
   a) Before you can tackle the problem of rubbish on the streets of your community you need to identify the problem areas. It's possible that there is rubbish all over the place but are there particular areas which are always heavily littered? For example, are there always lots of sweet wrappers in the area around the local sweet shop? You might:
   - draw a simple map of the area around your community
   - grade areas from 1 (seldom much rubbish) to 5 (badly affected most of the time).
   b) As well as where, you also need to know what and how much. You might:
   - gather the rubbish from a sample area and analyse it. You might separate it into categories like: paper and cardboard, plastic, glass, etc.

FIG 4.63 Quantifying the problem

Science, Technology, Education and Mathematics (STEM) activities are included which present real-life problems to be investigated and resolved using your science and technology skills. These pages are called **Science in practice**.

Unit 1: Human body systems: the excretory system

Excretion ⟩⟩⟩

All of the many chemical processes that take place in an organism are collectively called the body metabolism. As a result of metabolism, waste products are formed in the cells. If these were not continually removed they would accumulate and poison the cells.

Excretion is the removal of metabolic waste products from the body of an organism.

In humans, waste products are formed by a number of processes. The main metabolic waste products are given in Table 1.1.

FIG 1.1 Our bodies are continually producing metabolic waste products which must be excreted

Waste product	How it is formed	Where it is produced	How it is excreted
Carbon dioxide	During cellular respiration	In all living cells	Gaseous exchange in the lungs
Water			Through the lungs and skin, and as urine and faeces
Urea	Deamination of unwanted amino acids	In the liver	As urea in urine and sweat
Bile pigments	Breakdown of old red blood cells		In the faeces

TABLE 1.1

The three organs mainly responsible for excretion in humans are the kidney, the lungs and the skin. The following flow chart summarises their roles.

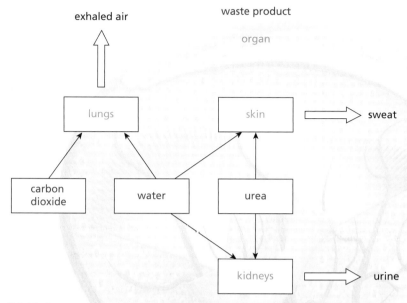

FIG 1.2 Organs responsible for excretion

Excretion is the removal of the waste products of metabolism from the body and not undigested food, which is removed by a different process called egestion. Egestion and excretion are different processes and should not be confused.

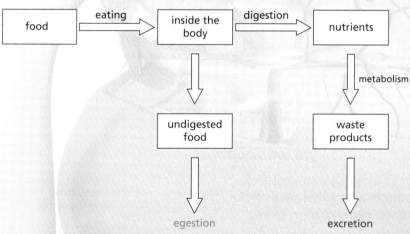

FIG 1.3 Egestion and excretion

Excretion by the kidneys

We are learning how to:

- identify location and parts of the kidneys
- understand how the kidneys filter our blood and remove substances.

Position of the kidneys ⟩⟩⟩

The kidneys remove waste products from the blood. These are stored in the bladder in solution as urine, ready to be excreted at regular intervals. The body has two kidneys situated in the lower abdomen. Each kidney is connected to the bladder by a tube called a **ureter**.

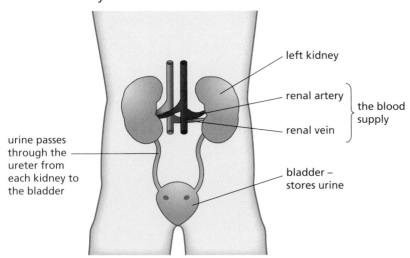

left kidney

renal artery
renal vein
} the blood supply

urine passes through the ureter from each kidney to the bladder

bladder – stores urine

FIG 1.4 Position of the kidneys

> **Something to think about**
>
> The kidneys are essential for life. People who have defective kidneys must have waste products removed from their blood regularly by **dialysis**. If they are lucky they might receive a replacement healthy kidney by a transplant operation.

Structure of the kidneys

Each kidney consists of two main regions – the cortex and the medulla. Running between these regions are structures called nephrons where waste products are removed from the blood.

The nephrons are responsible for removing a mixture of useful substances and waste products and substances from the blood by **ultrafiltration** and then reabsorbing useful substances by **selective reabsorption**.

Each nephron contains a knot of blood capillaries called a glomerulus. As blood is forced through these capillaries a solution called the filtrate is formed in Bowman's capsule. This contains a mixture of both useful substances and waste products.

As the filtrate passes around the loop of Henle, useful substances like amino acids, glucose and some mineral salts are reabsorbed back into the blood capillaries. The remainder passes out of the nephron into a collecting duct from which it goes to the bladder.

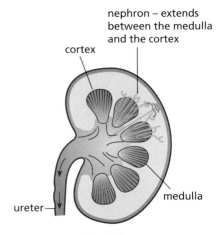

nephron – extends between the medulla and the cortex

cortex

medulla

ureter

FIG 1.5 Parts of the kidney

Activity 1.1

Observing the structure of a kidney

Here is what you need:
- goat's kidney
- scissors
- scalpel
- dissecting pins
- hand lens.

Here is what you should do:

1. Carefully examine the outside of the kidney. What shape is it? Observe where the kidney connects to the bladder via a ureter.

2. Cut the kidney in half longways and look at the inside. Can you see the cortex and the medulla regions? Can you see any other structures inside the kidney?

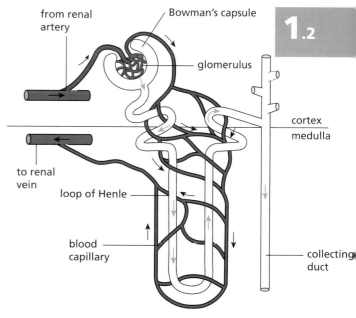

FIG 1.6 Structure of a nephron

Check your understanding

1. The following table shows the concentration of substances in blood plasma, in the filtrate obtained in Bowman's capsule and in urine.

Substance	% in blood plasma	% in filtrate	% in urine
Amino acids	0.05	0.05	0.0
Glucose	0.1	0.1	0.0
Proteins	7.0	0.0	0.0
Salts	0.45	0.45	0.80
Urea	0.03	0.04	2.0

a) Which substance is not removed from the blood plasma during ultrafiltration?

b) Which two substances are removed from blood plasma by ultrafiltration and are not reabsorbed by selective reabsorption? Explain how you can tell this from the figures in the table.

Key terms

ureter tube that connects a kidney to the bladder along which urine passes

ultrafiltration the removal of a mixture of useful substances and waste products as the filtrate in the glomerulus

selective reabsorption the reabsorption of useful substances as the filtrate passes through the loop of Henle

dialysis removal of metabolism waste products outside the body by machine

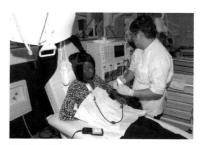

FIG 1.7 Dialysis

The roles of the lungs and the skin in excretion

We are learning how to:

- understand how and what our lungs excrete
- measure which parts of our bodies sweat the most.

Excretion in the lungs ⟫

We think of the lungs as the organ that provides the body with oxygen but they also have an important role to play in excretion.

The oxygen absorbed by the lungs, and the glucose obtained by digestion, are carried around the body in the blood. They are required for the process of **respiration** which provides cells with energy:

glucose + oxygen → carbon dioxide + water + energy

The waste products of respiration are carbon dioxide and water. If these were not continually removed from a cell the cell would soon cease to function. For example, carbon dioxide dissolves in water to give an acidic solution. If it was not removed from the cell it would lower the pH of the cytoplasm, which would interfere with other chemical reactions.

Carbon dioxide and water are carried away in the blood and excreted in the lungs. Exhaled air contains about 4% carbon dioxide and is always saturated with water vapour.

During deamination the $-NH_2$ group is removed from the amino acid forming NH_3 (ammonia). The remainder of the amino acid molecule is converted to carbohydrates to provide the body with energy:

$$CO_2 + NH_3 \rightarrow CO(NH_2)_2 \text{ (urea)}$$

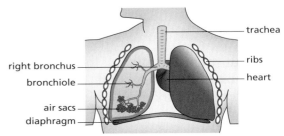

right bronchus

bronchiole

air sacs

diaphragm

trachea

ribs

heart

FIG 1.8 Structure of the lungs

Activity 1.2

Investigating which parts of the body sweat most

Here is what you will need:

- blue cobalt chloride paper – squares × 6
- access to a watch or clock.

Here is what you should do:

1. Mark each piece of blue cobalt chloride paper with a number from 1 to 6.

Formation of urea

Urea is formed in the liver as a result of the deamination of amino acids. The body cannot use all of the amino acids obtained from food to build new proteins.

2. Decide six places on your body which you are going to compare for the amount of sweat produced. List which number goes with which body part.

3. Go and stand somewhere warm so that you are sweating.

4. Place the first piece of blue cobalt chloride paper on a part of your body for example, your forehead. Leave it there for a few minutes until you can see it turning pink. The length of time will depend on how much you are sweating. Make a note of the time.

5. Repeat step 4 on the remaining five parts of your body using the same time period as you did for the first one.

6. Compare how much each cobalt chloride paper turned pink. Deduce which part of your body sweated more and which sweated least.

> **Fun fact**
>
> Cobalt chloride paper is blue when anhydrous but turns pink in the presence of water. It can be used to detect the presence of water.

Ammonia is toxic so it is combined with carbon dioxide to form urea, which is less toxic and is removed from the body in urine and sweat.

Excretion through the skin

The skin is the largest organ of the body and has many functions, including the excretion of urea and water.

Within the skin there are many **sweat glands** leading to pores on the surface. It is through these pores that the body loses sweat. **Sweat** consists mostly of water but it also contains small amounts of dissolved substances such as urea and minerals.

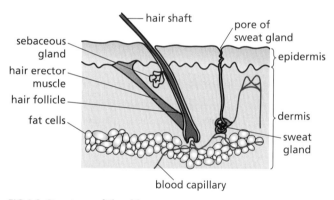

FIG 1.9 Structure of the skin

Sweating serves two important purposes for the body:

- it allows the body to excrete water and urea
- when the water from sweat evaporates it cools the body.

After the water from sweat has evaporated small amounts of solids like urea are left behind, which is why people smell if they do not wash regularly.

Check your understanding

1. State from which organ(s) each of the following are excreted.

   a) carbon dioxide   b) urea   c) water.

> **Key terms**
>
> **respiration** process by which cells obtain energy
>
> **sweat gland** structure in the skin through which sweat is released
>
> **sweat** water containing small amounts of dissolved solids like urea and mineral salts

Water balancing

We are learning how to:

• spot the signs of dehydration.

The human body loses water in a number of different ways including:

• as urine – a solution of waste products such as urea and mineral salts

• as sweat – essentially water but contains some urea and mineral salts.

Sweating

Sweating is an important mechanism in maintaining the body at a constant temperature. As the water from sweat evaporates from the skin it removes heat and so it helps to cool the body.

The amount a person sweats is determined by the temperature of their surroundings and how active they are.

When the weather is hot or when a person is very active, perhaps playing a sport, their body gets hot. They produce lots of sweat in order to cool down to maintain body temperature.

When the weather is cool or a person is inactive, perhaps sitting reading a book, they produce very little sweat. The body doesn't need to lose heat in order to maintain body temperature.

The body loses far more water through sweating on a hot day than it does on a cold day. If the body produced the same amount of urine on a hot day as it does on a cold day, the person would soon become **dehydrated** and feel unwell. So how does the body control the amount of urine produced?

Action of the kidneys

The kidney maintains water balance by varying the amount of water reabsorbed into the blood. This results in urine of different **concentrations**.

dilute ← → concentrated

FIG 1.11 Urine changes colour with concentration

> ### Something to think about
>
> When the urine is deep yellow or orange this is a sign that the body is dehydrated and the person must drink some water straight away.

FIG 1.10 On hot days we lose lots of water through sweating

FIG 1.12 Sportspersons need to drink water to prevent becoming dehydrated

On hot days or when a person is active they produce lots of sweat. Their kidneys compensate for this by reabsorbing lots of water so less urine is produced. Their urine is highly coloured because the concentration of urea and other waste substances is high.

On cool days or when a person is inactive they produce very little sweat. Their kidneys reabsorb relatively little water so more urine is produced. Their urine is very pale because the concentration of urea and other substances is low.

Activity 1.3

Finding out about dehydration and oral rehydration solutions

You should work in a group of 3 or 4 for this activity. You are going to research into dehydration and how oral rehydration solutions (ORS) may be used to treat this condition.

In carrying out your research you should consider such things as:

- What is dehydration?

- When a person becomes dehydrated are they just short of water or is there more to it?

- Why might vomiting and/or diarrhoea result in dehydration?

- What do ORS contain?

- What brands of ORS are available at your local pharmacy?

- How should ORS be taken?

Prepare a brief oral report on dehydration that you can present to the class.

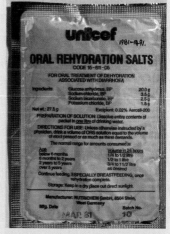

FIG 1.13 Oral rehydration salts

Check your understanding

1. The following table shows the amount of water lost by a person in different ways during a cool day.

Way in which water was lost	Volume / cm³
From the lungs	650
From the skin	550
In faeces	250
As urine	1250

a) Show this data as a bar graph.

b) Describe how the amounts of water lost by the different ways will change on a hot day.

Key terms

dehydrated containing less water that normal

concentration amount of a substance dissolved in a given volume of liquid

Review of Human body systems: the excretory system

- Excretion is the removal of the waste products of metabolism from the body.

- Metabolic waste products include carbon dioxide, water and urea.

- Egestion is a different process to excretion and is the removal of undigested food from the body.

- The kidneys absorb waste products from the blood which eventually pass out of the body as urine.

- Each kidney consists of an outer cortex and an inner medulla.

- In a nephron ultrafiltration removes useful and waste substances from the blood and the useful substances are reabsorbed.

- Dialysis is a method of removing waste from the blood artificially using a machine.

- Carbon dioxide and water vapour are excreted by the lungs.

- Water and urea are excreted by the skin as sweat.

- Heat is lost from the body when the water in sweat evaporates.

- People produce lots of sweat on hot days and/or when they are active.

- People produce little sweat on cool days and/or when they are inactive.

- The kidneys control water loss from the body by producing more or less urine.

- Dilute urine is pale while concentrated urine is coloured yellow-orange.

- Oral rehydration salts are used to treat dehydration.

Review questions on Human body systems: the excretory system

1. a) How is egestion different from excretion?

   b) Name three organs concerned with excretion.

2. The following diagram shows a section through a kidney.

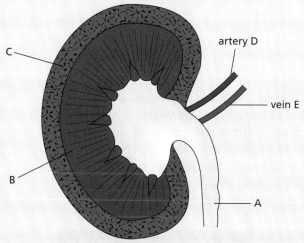

FIG 1.14

   a) Name parts A, B and C.

   b) State one way that the blood in vein E differs from that in artery D.

   c) What passes along A and where does it go?

3. Justin has noticed that after playing football for an hour on a sunny day his urine is a much deeper colour than normal.

   a) Explain why this is the case.

   b) How can Justin make his urine return to its normal colour?

4. a) What is a glomerulus and in which part of a nephron is it found?

   b) What happens during ultrafiltration?

   c) What happens during selective reabsorption?

   d) Why don't blood proteins pass out of the blood during ultrafiltration?

5. In terms of water loss from the body, what difference, if any, would you expect to each of the following on a hot day compared to a cool day?

   a) Amount of sweat produced.

   b) Amount of water in exhaled air.

   c) Colour of urine.

   d) Amount of urine.

Unit 2: Human body systems: the reproductive system

Reproduction »»

Reproduction is one of the seven characteristics of all living things. Reproduction is the means by which a species continues to exist. Organisms exhibit a number of different methods of reproduction, for example sexual reproduction or asexual reproduction. In humans, sexual reproduction takes place. This occurs between a male and a female and requires specialised reproductive systems.

FIG 2.1 Male and female

The male sex cells are called sperm and the female sex cells are called ova (singular ovum). For reproduction to occur, the sperm must leave the male body and enter the female, where it joins an ovum and fertilisation takes place. This results in the formation of an embryo, which grows inside the female.

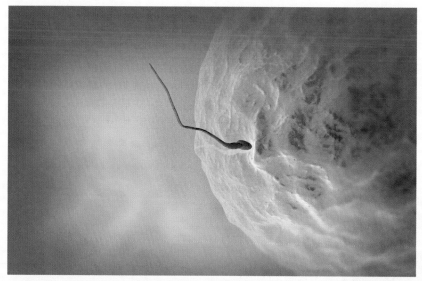

FIG 2.2 A sperm fertilises an ovum

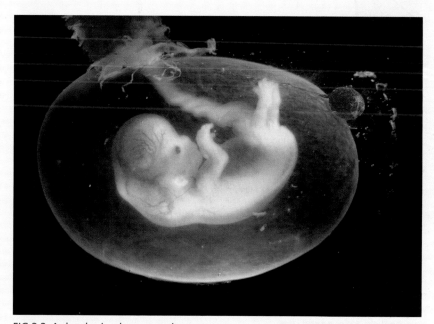

FIG 2.3 A developing human embryo

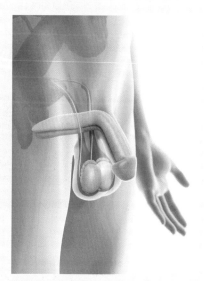

FIG 2.4 The human male reproductive system

Because the male and female reproductive systems have different functions, they are different in structure. In this unit you will learn about the structure of both systems and how the structure of each relates to their functions.

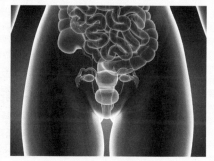

FIG 2.5 The human female reproductive system

The male reproductive system

We are learning how to:

- outline the structure of the human male and female reproductive systems and the functions of the parts
- identify the parts of the male reproductive system and their functions.

The male reproductive system »»

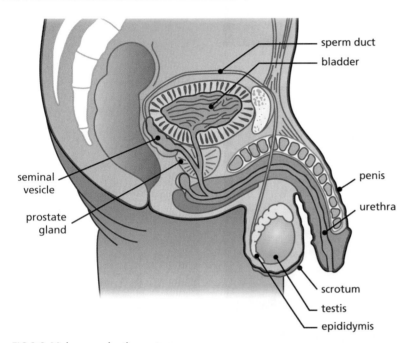

FIG 2.6 Male reproductive system

The male reproductive organs are the two **testes**. These lie outside the body cavity in a sac called the **scrotum**. This allows the testes to remain at a temperature that is slightly below normal body temperature. This favours the production of **sperm**.

Each testis contains many tubes in which sperm is formed. These meet and join to connect with the epididymis.

The epididymis leads to the **sperm duct**. The two sperm ducts open into the ureter just after it leaves the bladder. Urine from the bladder and sperm both pass out of the **penis** through the urethra. The body has a mechanism that prevents these events happening at the same time.

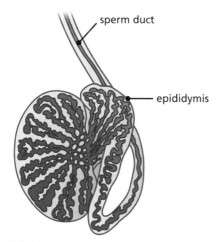

sperm duct

epididymis

FIG 2.7 Structure of a testis

The seminal vesicle branches from each sperm duct just before it enters the prostate gland. The seminal vesicle contains fluid that mixes with the sperm to form semen. The prostate gland secretes a fluid that nourishes the sperm. Millions of sperm are released each time a male ejaculates.

Activity 2.1

Tracing the movement of sperm

Here is what you need:

- model of the male reproductive organs (if this is not available use Fig 2.6).

Here is what you should do:

1. Follow the passage of the sperm from where it is formed to where it leaves the body on the model.

2. Make a list of the parts of the male reproductive system in the order that sperm passes through them.

Check your understanding

1. In which parts of the male reproductive system is sperm produced?

2. What is the function of the seminal vesicles?

3. What is the name of the duct that joins the epididymis to the urethra?

4. What else apart from sperm leaves the body through the urethra?

Fun fact

A vasectomy is a procedure a man can have if he and his partner agree that they do not want to have any more children. It involves a minor operation during which a short section of each sperm duct is removed and the remaining ends tied off. This prevents sperm from passing from the testes to the urethra. A vasectomy does not affect a man's ability to have sexual intercourse.

Key terms

testes male reproductive organs

scrotum sac outside the body that contains the testes

sperm specialised reproductive cells produced in the testes

sperm duct tube along which sperm pass before they reach the prostate gland

penis part of male reproductive system through which sperm and urine pass

The female reproductive system

We are learning how to:

- outline the structure of the human male and female reproductive systems and the functions of the parts
- identify the parts of the female reproductive system and their functions.

The female reproductive system

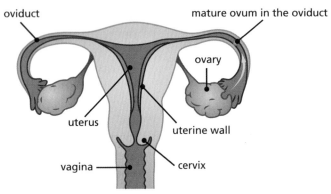

FIG 2.8 All of the parts of the female system are held within the body cavity

The female reproductive organs are two **ovaries**. These are found at the back of the abdomen, just below the kidneys. **Ova** develop in the ovaries.

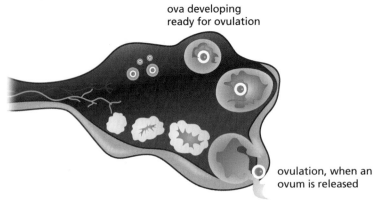

FIG 2.9 Structure of an ovary

When a female is mature, her ovaries will release one ovum each month. This is called **ovulation**.

Fun fact

Men produce new sperm daily throughout their lives. Women are born with all of their ova. These are in the form of immature ova or follicles, which are stored in the ovaries.

A woman will have between one and two million follicles at birth. Of these, only about 400 will mature during the woman's child-conceiving years, while the rest will die.

When a woman can no longer have children, few or no follicles will remain in her ovaries.

Close to each ovary is the funnel-shaped opening of an oviduct. The oviducts are also called **fallopian tubes**. They are narrow tubes along which the ova pass from the ovaries to the **uterus**. Fertilisation of an ovum by a sperm normally happens in the oviduct.

The uterus is wider than the oviducts. It is the place where a fertilised ovum will develop into an embryo and eventually into a baby.

The uterus, which is usually about 80 mm long, connects with the outside of the body by a muscular tube called the **vagina**. The neck of the uterus is a ring of muscle called the **cervix**.

The urethra, which carries urine from the bladder, opens at the outer end of the vagina.

Activity 2.2

Tracing the movement of ova

Here is what you need:

- model of the female reproductive organs (if this is not available use Fig 2.8).

Here is what you should do:

1. Follow the passage of the ova from where they are formed to where they leave the body (assuming they are not fertilised) on the model.

2. Make a list of the parts of the female reproductive system in the order that the ova pass through them.

Check your understanding

1. In which parts of the female reproductive system are ova produced?

2. What is the name of the duct that joins an ovary to the uterus?

3. What is the cervix and where is it found?

4. How many ova are normally released at one time?

Key terms

ovaries female reproductive organs

ova specialised female reproductive cells

ovulation when a mature female releases one ovum each month

fallopian tubes narrow tubes along which the ova pass from the ovaries to the uterus

uterus the place where a fertilised ovum will develop into an embryo and eventually into a baby

vagina muscular tube connecting the uterus with the outside of the body

cervix ring of muscle where the uterus joins the vagina

Review of Human body systems: the reproductive system

- The testes are the male reproductive organs. They are found in the scrotum outside the body cavity.

- Sperm is produced in many tubes inside the testes. These tubes meet and join to connect with the epididymis. During ejaculation sperm passes from the testes through the sperm ducts into the urethra, and leaves the body.

- As sperm passes along the sperm duct it mixes with a fluid from the seminal vesicle to form semen, and is nourished by fluid from the prostate gland.

- The ovaries are the female reproductive organs. They release an ovum once each month. The ovum passes along an oviduct into the uterus. If the ovum is fertilised by a sperm this normally takes place in the oviduct. The fertilised ovum will become embedded in the uterus wall and develop into a baby.

- If the ovum is not fertilised, it will pass down the uterus, through the cervix into the vagina, and eventually leave the body.

Review questions on Human body systems: the reproductive system

1. Name the parts A to E in Fig 2.10.

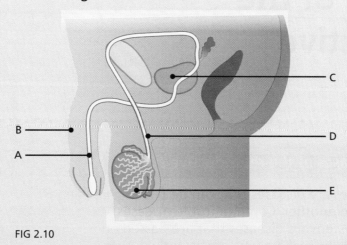

FIG 2.10

2. Name the parts A to E in Fig 2.11.

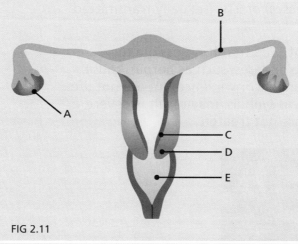

FIG 2.11

3. a) In which part of the body are the following formed:

    i) Sperm?

    ii) Ova?

  b) What travels along:

    i) an oviduct?

    ii) a sperm duct?

  c) What is the alternative name for a fallopian tube?

  d) How many of the following are normally released by the body at any one time:

    i) Sperm?

    ii) Ova?

Unit 3: Communicable diseases of the reproductive system

Communicable diseases of the reproductive system ⟫⟫

Communicable diseases are diseases that can be passed on from one person to another. Communicable diseases of the reproductive system are diseases that are passed on between people during sexual activity, particularly during sexual intercourse. These are sometimes called STDs (sexually transmitted diseases) or STIs (sexually transmitted infections).

There are several different STDs that it is possible for humans to contract. Some diseases, such as herpes, cause considerable discomfort and inconvenience but are not life-threatening. Others, such as syphilis, may result in severe illness and death if they are not treated.

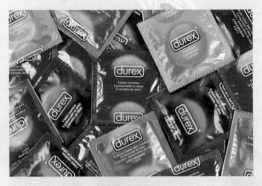

FIG 3.1 The transmission of sexually transmitted diseases is preventable if people are prepared to take sensible precautions, such as using condoms

Condoms provide a simple way of preventing the transfer of STDs, although they are not considered by doctors to be 100 per cent safe. Their effectiveness depends on them being used properly and not being damaged.

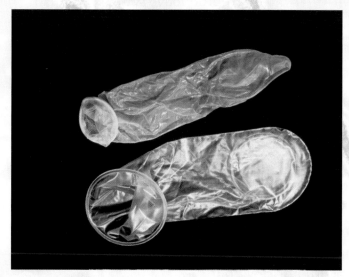

FIG 3.2 Male and female condoms

Both male and female condoms are available. The male condom is slipped over the penis prior to sexual intercourse, whereas the female condom is inserted into the vagina.

Despite the huge advantages of using female condoms, both as a contraceptive and to prevent the transmission of STDs, a surprisingly large proportion of females are unaware they exist and relatively few females use them compared to the use of the male condom.

If a person has any suspicion at all that he or she might be suffering from a disease of the reproductive system, it is important to seek medical advice straight away (it is far better to face a little embarrassment than to suffer the effects of a disease and to pass on the disease to other people).

Each year, a significant proportion of the country's resources is spent on dealing with problems resulting from diseases of the reproductive system.

There are a number of local agencies, such as the Family Planning Association of Trinidad and Tobago, that will provide advice about STDs. If you believe you have contracted an STD, they will carry out tests to check if this is the case and can advise about treatment.

Something to think about

There is a lot of misinformation about sexually transmitted diseases. People who do not know very much try to hide their ignorance by making up stories or repeating the stories of others.

There is a lot of reliable information on the internet about sexually transmitted diseases and there are clinics where you can obtain information and talk to informed people. Here is an example of a website you could try:

kidshealth.org/teen/sexual_health/

Herpes, chlamydia and human papilloma virus (HPV)

We are learning how to:

- identify the different types of communicable diseases of the reproductive system
- describe herpes, chlamydia and human papilloma virus (HPV).

Herpes, chlamydia and human papilloma virus (HPV) ⟩⟩⟩

Herpes simplex virus (HSV)

Herpes is caused by the herpes simplex virus (HSV).

Genital herpes is a common STD that results in blisters around the genitals of both men and women.

Herpes can be treated with the **antiviral drug** Aciclovir but the virus stays in the body and can recur.

Chlamydia

Chlamydia is caused by the bacterium *Chlamydia trachomatis*. Most people who have chlamydia do not experience any symptoms.

Chlamydia is treated with antibiotics.

Human papilloma virus (HPV)

The **human papilloma virus (HPV)** is a group of viruses that affect the skin and the moist linings of your body.

HPV is a highly contagious infection. There is no medical cure for the condition but the body's immune system is usually able to deal with it.

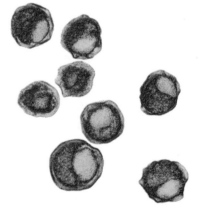

FIG 3.3 The bacterium *Chlamydia trachomatis*

Activity 3.1

Researching bacterial vaginosis

You will not require any equipment or materials for this activity, but you will need sources of reference material.

Here is what you should do:

Carry out research into the disease bacterial vaginosis. Use these questions to help you structure your answer.

1. What causes this disease?
2. What are the symptoms of this disease?

3. How are people infected?

4. What is the cure for this disease?

Check your understanding

1. The following passage is about a common STD called trichomoniasis. Read it carefully and answer the questions that follow.

FIG 3.4 *Trichomonas vaginalis* parasite

Trichomoniasis or 'trich' is caused by the protozoan parasite called Trichomonas vaginalis. *The parasite is passed from an infected person to an uninfected person during unprotected sex.*

Most women and men who have the parasite are not aware that they are infected.

When trichomoniasis does cause symptoms, they can range from mild irritation to severe inflammation. Men may feel itching or irritation inside the penis. There may also be burning after urination or ejaculation. Women may notice itching and discomfort during urination. They may also experience burning, redness or soreness of the genitals. The infection can be successfully treated with antibiotics.

  a) What causes the disease?

  b) Why might a person not realise that they are infected?

  c) How is the disease passed from person to person?

  d) What symptoms might an infected man experience?

  e) How is the disease treated?

Something to think about

Some STDs often produce few or no symptoms. People may have the disease for a long period of time and not be aware of it. During this time they might be infecting other people.

Key terms

herpes a sexually transmitted disease caused by the herpes simplex virus (HSV)

antiviral drug a drug that treats a virus

chlamydia one of the most common STDs, it is caused by the bacterium *Chlamydia trachomatis*

human papilloma virus (HPV) a group of viruses that affect the skin and the moist linings of the body

Gonorrhoea, syphilis and HIV

We are learning how to:

- explain the transmission of HIV (human immunodeficiency virus)
- describe gonorrhoea, syphilis and HIV.

Gonorrhoea, syphilis and HIV ⟫⟫

Gonorrhoea

Gonorrhoea is sometimes known simply as 'the clap'.

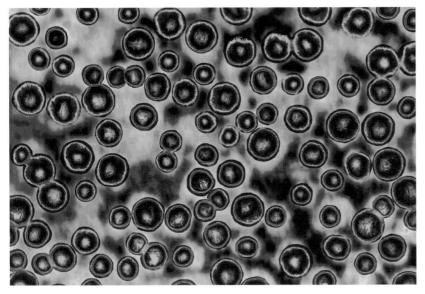

FIG 3.5 Gonorrhoea is caused by a bacterium called *Neisseria gonorrhoeae* or *gonococcus*

The typical symptoms of gonorrhoea include a thick green or yellow discharge from the vagina or penis, pain when urinating, and bleeding between periods in women.

The disease is usually treated with a single **antibiotic** injection and a single antibiotic tablet. If it is not treated there is a risk of serious complications, including infertility (inability to have children).

Syphilis

Syphilis is caused by a bacterium that is readily passed from an infected person during sexual activity.

There are three stages in the development of syphilis.

1. Primary syphilis: to begin with the disease is painless but there are highly infectious sores around the genitals. These last between two and six weeks before disappearing.

Fun fact

A number of famous people from history are thought to have died from syphilis, including Christopher Columbus, who was the first European to discover Trinidad, on July 31 1498.

FIG 3.6 Christopher Columbus

Scientists can never be certain without examining the person's body, but observations made by physicians, especially at the time a person was ill and died, sometimes correspond closely with the symptoms observed during the latter stages of untreated syphilis.

2. Secondary syphilis: the person remains infectious and develops symptoms such as skin rashes and a sore throat. These quickly disappear. After this the person will experience no other symptoms, perhaps for a number of years.

3. Tertiary syphilis: around one third of infected people who are not treated will, sooner or later, develop serious conditions, including heart disease, blindness, deafness, paralysis, insanity and eventual death.

Syphilis is treated using antibiotics, usually in the form of penicillin injections.

HIV and AIDS

AIDS stands for acquired immune deficiency syndrome. It is caused by a virus called the human immunodeficiency virus, or **HIV**.

The virus attacks the body's immune system, which is responsible for fighting diseases. This leaves the body unable to destroy the germs that cause other diseases.

You will learn a lot more about HIV and AIDS in future lessons.

Check your understanding

Answer the following questions about syphilis.

1. What type of organism causes syphilis?

2. During which stages is it infectious?

3. Why might a person who has contracted syphilis incorrectly think they are no longer infected?

4. What is the usual treatment for this disease?

Key terms

gonorrhoea sexually transmitted disease caused by bacterium called *Neisseria gonorrhoeae* or *gonococcus*

antibiotic medicine that works on bacterial infections

syphilis sexually transmitted disease caused by a bacterium that is readily passed from an infected person during sexual activity

AIDS stands for acquired immune deficiency syndrome

HIV human immunodeficiency virus, the virus that can cause AIDS

Transmission and prevention of STDs

We are learning how to:

- identify the different types of communicable diseases of the reproductive system
- describe ways of preventing STDs.

Transmission and prevention of STDs

Diseases are described as sexually transmitted when they are passed from one person to another during sexual activity and, in particular, during sexual intercourse.

These diseases spread most rapidly when people have sexual relationships with a number of different partners and when they have unprotected sex, that is sex without a condom.

FIG 3.7 Long-term partners

The simplest way to avoid STDs is not to have any sort of sexual relationship, until you are with a long-term partner and you both know that the other is not infected nor likely to be sexually active with others. The chances of becoming infected are much reduced if a person only has sex with one partner, in a stable relationship.

One of the most widely used methods of protection against STDs or STIs is **condoms.** They are available for both males and females. The condom provides a barrier between the **body fluids** of the participants during intercourse so tiny organisms such as viruses and bacteria cannot pass from one person to the other.

FIG 3.8 Condoms provide some protection from STDs if they are used consistently and correctly

Having unprotected sex just once can be enough for a disease to be passed on from one person to another. People who suspect they have been infected can go to a **clinic**, where they will be examined and tests will be done. If treatment is necessary they will be given suitable drugs.

STD clinics can provide help to cure these diseases but it is much better not to contract them in the first place. Many people end up suffering from an STD simply through lack of knowledge.

Avoidance of STDs is better than cure.

Activity 3.2

Informing people about STDs

Here is what you need:

- leaflets, pamphlets and other information available from STD and other clinics
- large sheet of paper or thin card.

Here is what you should do:

Use the printed material you obtain to make a poster informing people about one or more STDs and telling them how to avoid becoming infected.

Check your understanding

1. A young adult claims to have had unprotected sexual intercourse with several different partners and never caught any STDs. He thinks that all of the warnings about STDs are unnecessary.

   Do you agree with this opinion? What can you say that you think might persuade him to reconsider his attitude and become more socially responsible?

Fun fact

There are a number of health centres that provide healthcare and counselling to people with sexually transmitted diseases.

The services provided by these centres include: clinic care, counselling, blood tests for STDs and HIV/AIDS, treatment for STDs and referrals for further care where necessary.

Some centres have a walk-in service, which means you do not need to make an appointment, and it is free to all citizens of Trinidad and Tobago.

Key terms

condoms a barrier between the fluids of the participants during intercourse so organisms cannot pass from one person to the other

body fluids fluids such as semen that are discharged by the body

clinic place where medical advice is given

avoidance stopping yourself from getting a disease

HIV and AIDS

We are learning how to:

- identify the different types of communicable diseases of the reproductive system
- understand the difference between HIV and AIDS.

HIV and AIDS >>>

HIV

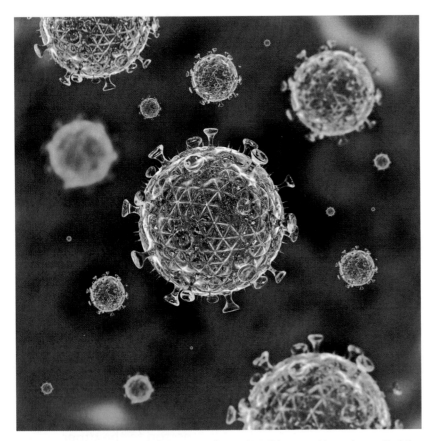

FIG 3.9 Acquired immune deficiency syndrome (AIDS) is caused by a virus called the human immunodeficiency virus (HIV)

The body's immune system defends it against disease. If the germs that cause a disease enter the body, the immune system can destroy them so you do not become ill.

HIV attacks the white blood cells, which are an important part of the body's immune system. Once the immune system is not working properly, the body is open to attack by germs that can cause a whole range of illnesses.

HIV lives only within cells and body fluids, not outside the body. HIV does not attack the body, but it weakens its defences. A person infected with HIV may not show any symptoms for a number of years but the immune system gradually becomes weaker, leaving the person more susceptible to infection.

AIDS

AIDS is described as a **syndrome** rather than a disease, because it manifests itself in the body as a whole collection of diseases that all result from a weakening of the immune system.

The first symptoms of AIDS are very much like flu. They include a high temperature and swollen glands.

As the body's immune system becomes weaker, the body may develop more serious conditions like pneumonia and different types of cancer. It is these conditions that will eventually cause the person to die.

Activity 3.3

National Strategic Plan 2013–2018

You should work in a small group for this activity. You will not need any equipment or materials but you will need access to the internet.

Here is what you should do:

As part of the HIV and AIDS National Strategic Plan 2013–2018, the government has created an information website at hiv.health.gov.tt/

Investigate this website and find out how it helps people to find out more about HIV/AIDS.

Check your understanding

1. Why can the germs that cause minor illnesses in healthy people make people with AIDS very ill?

Medical fact

The first recognised cases of AIDS occurred in the USA in the early 1980s. The first case in the Caribbean was reported in Jamaica in 1982.

Key term

syndrome a medical condition that has a range of effects

3.5

Ways of contracting HIV/AIDS

We are learning how to:

- explain the transmission of HIV (human immunodeficiency virus)
- understand different ways in which a person may contract HIV.

Ways of contracting HIV/AIDS ›››

There are three main ways in which a person might contract HIV.

Unprotected sexual intercourse

HIV can be spread as a result of sexual contact. In particular, the virus can be transferred during unprotected vaginal or anal intercourse.

Infected blood

People in hospital sometimes receive a **blood transfusion**. Blood used in blood transfusions is given by blood donors.

A person who has HIV is said to be HIV positive. If a person who is HIV positive has not developed AIDS, they may not realise that they are carrying the virus.

Before scientists realised the virus could be passed on in blood, people who were HIV positive were able to be blood donors. When their blood was given in a transfusion, the recipient became infected with the virus. Blood used in transfusions is now checked so HIV can no longer be transmitted this way.

Drug addicts may pass on HIV by sharing needles.

From an infected mother

If a pregnant woman is HIV positive, it is possible that her child will be born HIV positive because the virus can transfer across the placenta during pregnancy. The baby could also acquire the virus from the mother during delivery or through breast milk.

A mother who has HIV will not necessarily pass the infection on to her baby.

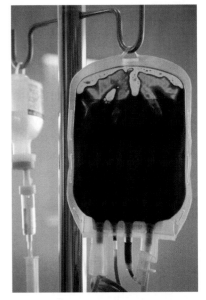

FIG 3.10 Blood used in blood transfusions is given by blood donors

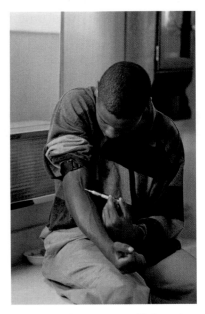

FIG 3.11 A tiny amount of infected blood left on a needle is enough to infect another person

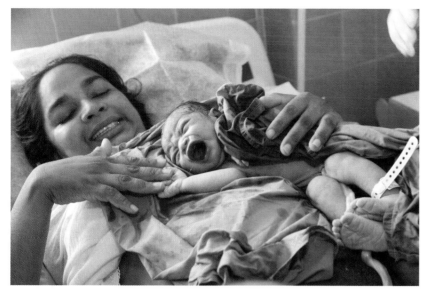

FIG 3.12 Newborn babies can be at risk of infection from many sources

Role-play about the transmission of STDs

You will need to work in a small group for this activity. You will not need any equipment or materials but you will have to use objects to improvise.

Here is what you should do:

Devise roleplay situations that may be responsible for the transmission of communicable sexual diseases. In each case, highlight how a person might protect themselves.

Check your understanding

1. Explain each of the following as fully as you can.

   a) Drug addicts should not use shared needles to inject themselves with drugs.

   b) Donated blood is tested for different things before it is considered safe to use.

   c) A person might be HIV positive even though they have not been sexually active or used drugs.

Fun fact

Medical people wear thin latex gloves as a matter of course when treating patients where there is the possibility of coming into contact with their blood or other body fluids.

FIG 3.13 The latex provides a barrier that prevents the wearer from becoming infected

The layer of latex is essential for protection; rubber or plastic gloves are not suitable or effective for this purpose.

Key terms

blood transfusion procedure where a patient who has lost a lot of their own blood, as a result of an accident or surgery or similar, is given some blood donated by another person

drug addicts people who are addicted to drugs such as heroin

Living with HIV/AIDS

We are learning how to:

- discuss strategies for protecting oneself against HIV infection
- understand and empathise with the problems experienced by those who must live with HIV and AIDS.

Living with HIV/AIDS »

Although there are drugs that can reduce the impact of AIDS, there is currently no known cure for this syndrome. People who are infected with HIV will remain so for the rest of their lives.

It is *not* possible to get AIDS by:

- kissing
- touching (for example, hugging or shaking hands with) a sufferer
- breathing the same air as a sufferer
- touching the same object as a sufferer
- insect bites.

Unfortunately, many AIDS sufferers are rejected by other members of their community because of false information. At a time when the sufferer needs support to come to terms with what has happened to them, their friends and, sometimes, even their family members do not visit them.

AIDS sufferers sometimes lose their jobs and their ability to support their family because their work colleagues are frightened that they will catch the syndrome. The AIDS victim then has no alternative but to rely on charity to survive.

AIDS

Don't be afraid, be aware.

FIG 3.14 The natural fear that people have about catching any disease is greatly magnified with HIV because there is no cure and the future prospects for a person who does become infected are not good

Activity 3.5

Educating people about AIDS sufferers

Here is what you need:

- large sheet of paper or thin card
- paints or colouring pencils.

Here is what you should do:

Many of the problems experienced by AIDS sufferers are due to people in their community not having enough information about the syndrome. This lack of knowledge causes people to be frightened.

Your task is to design a poster that will educate people in the community about some of the misconceptions about AIDS.

FIG 3.15 AIDS support groups consist of sufferers and non-sufferers who get together to help each other

In communities that have a sensible and well-informed approach to dealing with the problems caused by AIDS, there may be support groups. Members of support groups talk about the problems caused by AIDS openly, and share the things that they have found helpful in dealing with them.

Check your understanding

1. List and explain some of the problems that may be experienced by people living with HIV/AIDS.

> **Medical fact**
>
> In 2013 it was estimated that around 14 000 adults over the age of 15 were living with HIV in Trinidad and Tobago. The number is divided approximately equally between males and females.

Review of Communicable diseases of the reproductive system

- Communicable diseases of the reproductive system are often called sexually transmitted diseases (STDs) or sexually transmitted infections (STIs). These diseases are described as sexually transmitted because they may be transmitted from one person to another during sexual activity, and in particular sexual intercourse.

- Herpes, chlamydia and the human papilloma virus (HPV) are examples of common STDs.

Disease	Cause	Symptoms/Effects	Treatment
Genital herpes	virus	skin damage or blisters round the genitals	antiviral drug Aciclovir
Chlamydia	bacterium	number of symptoms, though some sufferers may be unaware that they have it	antibiotics
Human papilloma virus	group of viruses	affects moist membranes of body – may lead to genital warts and cervical cancer in women if left untreated	no medical treatment but body's immune system is usually able to deal with it
Gonorrhoea	bacterium	thick green or yellow discharge from vagina or penis	antibiotics
Syphilis	bacterium	sores on the genitals – if not treated serious conditions such as heart disease, blindness, deafness, paralysis and insanity may develop	antibiotics, e.g. penicillin

TABLE 3.1

- The simplest way to avoid STDs is not to have any sort of sexual relationship unless you are with a long term partner and you each know that the other is not infected or likely to be sexually active with other people.

- Condoms provide some protection against STDs by preventing the transfer of body fluids.

- Many people end up with an STD because they lack knowledge. The number of cases of STDs each year can be reduced by educating people. It is better to avoid becoming infected even if there is a simple cure.

- HIV stands for human immunodeficiency virus and AIDS stands for acquired immune deficiency syndrome. HIV attacks the body's immune system and leaves it deficient or weakened so that it cannot destroy the germs that cause other diseases. People who develop AIDS die from a variety of diseases that attack their weakened body.

- People who have HIV are described as HIV positive. There are three main ways in which a person might acquire the virus:

  1. As a result of unprotected sex with someone who has the virus.

  2. As a result of receiving contaminated blood. This might happen when drug addicts share a needle to inject themselves.

  3. The virus can be passed from an infected mother to her baby during pregnancy, birth or afterwards during breastfeeding.

- There are a number of myths surrounding HIV/AIDS that are the result of ignorance and fear of the disease. As a result of these, people who are HIV positive sometimes do not receive the support they need from their community. Support groups can help people to deal with the practical problems resulting from HIV.

Review questions on Communicable diseases of the reproductive system

1. **a)** What does the abbreviation STD stand for?
   b) State whether each of the following is caused by a bacterium or a virus.
      i) HIV
      ii) syphilis
      iii) chlamydia
      iv) genital herpes

2. Which of the following are true about HIV/AIDS and which are false? Write T or F for each one.
   a) AIDS is best described as a syndrome rather than a disease.
   b) A person who contracts HIV will show immediate signs of infection.
   c) A person can contract AIDS by kissing someone who is infected.
   d) AIDS sufferers are sometimes isolated by their communities.
   e) HIV is transmitted by a certain kind of mosquito.
   f) There is no known cure for HIV/AIDS.

3. The table shows the estimated number of people in Trinidad and Tobago living with HIV/AIDS in the period 2001 to 2010.

Year	Number of people living with HIV/AIDS
2001	7800
2002	7800
2003	17 000
2004	29 000
2005	29 000
2006	29 000
2007	29 000
2008	29 000
2009	14 000
2010	14 000

TABLE 3.2   (Source Index Mundi)

   a) Draw a bar graph to represent this information.
   b) Between which two years was the greatest rise in the number of people living with HIV/AIDS?

c) i) What was the largest number of people living with HIV/AIDS?

    ii) For how many years was there that number of people?

4. a) What causes gonorrhoea?

    b) What are the symptoms of this disease?

    c) What is the treatment for this disease?

    d) What complication might occur if gonorrhoea is left untreated?

5. a) Describe what effect the human immunodeficiency virus (HIV) has on the immune system.

    b) Explain why a person suffering from acquired immune deficiency syndrome (AIDS) may become ill and die from a disease that would have little effect on a normal healthy person.

6. Here is an extract from a newspaper article on STDs and the use of condoms. Read it carefully and answer the questions that follow.

Fêtes, scantily-clad gyrating women and alcohol galore. But this combination can lead to a deadly end – HIV and sexually transmitted diseases (STDs), including the human papilloma virus (HPV). And despite increased condom-awareness campaigns, specially targeted for the season, Dr Peter Gentle is warning that the popular latex contraceptive is far from safe.

"T&T is determined that condom sex is safe sex and that is absolutely stupid," he said. "The failure rate of condoms is cumulative, which means the more intercourse one has, the more chance of being infected." He said there was a failure rate of between ten and 25 per cent with condom use in preventing the spread of HIV.

"And with HPV the failure rate is as high as 80 per cent because the virus comes off your body outside of the area covered by the condom," he said.

                                                     (Trinidad & Tobago Guardian online Monday, April 13 2015)

    a) Which sexually transmitted diseases are mentioned?

    b) Why does the writer suggest that condoms cannot be relied on to provide totally safe sex?

    c) What is the failure rate for preventing the spread of HIV using a condom?

    d) What is likely to increase the failure rate for a person?

Unit 4: Environmental impact of human activities

Environmental impact of human activities »

There are many ways in which humans can affect and change environments. Some of these impacts are outlined here.

Exploiting natural resources

Environments far from human habitation, that have no resources worthy of exploitation, are relatively untouched by humans. Environments that have resources are often exploited to the extent that few plant and animal populations remain.

Genetically modified (GM) crops

Genetically modified, or GM, crops may produce higher food crop yields, but scientists believe they may also create environmental problems.

Invasive alien species (IAS)

Every area has communities of different plants and animals linked together in food webs. Numbers are controlled by such factors as availability of food and the number of organisms feeding in it.

If a plant or animal is introduced to a new environment where there is unlimited food and no natural enemies, the result is a massive increase in its numbers.

FIG 4.1 In 1979 swarms of Africanised honey bees migrated across to Trinidad from Venezuela and they still continue to fly into Trinidad, threatening human lives and livestock

FIG 4.2 Flock of scarlet ibis in the Caroni swamp in Trinidad, a wetland that provides a variety of habitats

Nature reserves

Nature reserves are areas where human activity is strictly controlled so the organisms that live there do not become endangered or threatened with extinction.

Deforestation

Large areas of forest are being cut down every year to provide wood and farmland.

Forests provide lots of different habitats. Once these habitats are lost, the organisms that occupied them are also lost.

Biodiversity

Biodiversity is a measure of the number of different kinds of organism in an area. Trinidad and Tobago has the highest level of biodiversity in the Caribbean. Keeping a high level of biodiversity requires maintaining and protecting lots of different habitats.

Threatened species

Although Trinidad and Tobago boasts a high level of biodiversity, it also has a number of species of plants and animals that now exist in small numbers and are threatened with extinction if positive action is not taken.

The greenhouse effect and global warming

As a result of increases in atmospheric carbon dioxide and some other gases, the surface temperature of the Earth is increasing. The increase in temperature is called global warming.

Biodegradable and non-biodegradable

Natural materials, such as vegetable waste, rot when left in the ground. They are described as biodegradable. Materials made by humans, such as glass and plastics, are often non-biodegradable. The build-up of non-biodegradable waste is a problem that our society must solve.

The three Rs

People can take three steps to reduce the amount of waste that they produce:

- Reduce – by eliminating those things that are not really necessary.

- Reuse – by using articles multiple times before they are thrown away.

- Recycle – by reusing materials to make new articles.

Something to think about

It is impossible for a population of any plant or animal to live in a habitat without making some sort of environmental impact.

In order to conserve the environment, people must look for ways of sharing with other organisms and ways of minimising the impact of their activities on other organisms. Is there a place near where you live or in the school compound that you think could be made really interesting by cleaning it up and introducing some different habitats?

Effects of human activities on the environment

We are learning how to:

- explain the impact of human activities on the local and global environment
- identify ways in which human activity impacts on the environment.

Effects of human activities on the environment »

Living on Earth brings about changes to the **environment**.

FIG 4.3 People have always cleared land for farming and cut down trees for buildings and firewood

When the number of people was small, **natural processes** soon repaired the damage. Trees quickly grew, smoke from fires was diluted many times in the air and waste materials that were produced by people were soon broken down by decomposer organisms, such as bacteria and fungi.

What is different now is the scale of these changes. The world **population** has shown a rapid increase over the past 50 years. Scientists believe it will reach 10 billion people by the year 2050.

FIG 4.4 The population of Port of Spain is around 60 000

A large population makes large demands on the environment.

- How much land is needed to build homes for these people?

- How much land must be cultivated to feed these people?

- How much waste gas is released into the air from fires and vehicles?

- How much waste do these people create?

Natural processes alone cannot repair the environmental damage caused by a large population. We must all find ways of reducing the environmental impact of our way of life.

Activity 4.1

Problems resulting from a population increase

You should work in a group for this activity. You will not need any equipment or materials.

Here is what you should do:

The population of Port of Spain more than tripled from 3000 in 1792 to 10 422 in 1797. Imagine you lived in Port of Spain at that time.

1. Discuss in your group how the rapid increase in people would impact on the environment.

2. Make a list of the ways in which you think the environment may have been damaged.

Check your understanding

1. Make a list of the ways in which you have an impact on the environment.

2. How do you think the estimated increase in population will impact on the environment?

Fun fact

In order to predict population growth, scientists take into account factors such as birth rates, life expectancy and migration into and out of a country.

The population of Trinidad and Tobago is expected to go down between 2015 and 2025. Can you suggest why?

Key terms

environment the world around us

natural processes processes that take place in nature without humans taking action

population the number of people that live in an area

Urbanisation

We are learning how to:

- explain the impact of human activities on the local and global environment
- appreciate the impact that people have on the environment as towns grow.

Urbanisation >>>

Features of a **rural** environment might include:

- areas of grassland and forests
- areas that have been cultivated
- lots of different types of plants and animals
- few buildings and roads
- a low population density (the number of people per square kilometre)
- peace and quiet.

FIG 4.5 A rural environment is what we find in the countryside

Compared to a **rural** environment, an **urban** environment is likely to have:

- fewer areas of grassland and forest
- fewer types of plants and animals
- lots of buildings and roads
- a high population density
- a lot of noise.

Urbanisation is the increase in the proportion of people in a country who live in urban environments, that is towns and cities. As the population grows, the proportion of people who live in towns increases. People move to towns for a variety of reasons, such as looking for work or so they can use facilities that are not available in the countryside.

FIG 4.6 An urban environment is what we find in towns and cities

FIG 4.7 **a)** Port of Spain in 1850 **b)** Port of Spain today
Towns like Port of Spain have changed greatly over the past century as
urbanisation has increased

Activity 4.2

Effects of urbanisation

You should carry out this activity in a small group. You will
not need any equipment or materials.

Here is what you should do:

1. Look at the pictures in Fig 4.7 that show how Port of
   Spain has changed over the last century.

2. Make a list of the things that you think will have
   increased.

3. Make a list of the things that you think might have
   decreased.

4. What effect do you think urbanisation has on the
   environment around a town?

Check your understanding

1. Write a sentence to predict how each of the
   following would change as a town gets bigger. Give
   one reason to support each prediction.

   a) The amount of atmospheric pollution

   b) The level of noise

   c) The area of trees and vegetation

   d) The numbers of different plants and animals

   e) The amount of food available for wild animals

Fun fact

Urbanisation in Trinidad
and Tobago was
estimated to be
13.7 per cent in 2011, the
last year in which it was
measured. The degree of
urbanisation is likely to
rise every year as more
people move to the
towns to live and work.

Key terms

rural in the countryside

urban relating to towns
and cities

Industry

We are learning how to:

- explain the impact of human activities on the local and global environment
- appreciate the impact of industry on the environment.

Industry >>>

Towns and cities are not just places where people live, but also where they work. Most of the damage to the environment from urbanisation is a result of increased **industry**.

FIG 4.8 Many of the industries that produce electricity, raw materials and the products needed by modern society also produce waste gases that pollute the atmosphere

The exhaust gases from car and truck engines also put waste gases into the air and cause **atmospheric pollution**.

Materials that are released into the environment, either accidently or deliberately, may cause severe damage to plants and animals.

FIG 4.9 An oil spillage at sea may be washed ashore and will not only kill seaweed and fish, but may also damage animals such as birds that feed on them

FIG 4.10 A sea duck covered in oil from a damaged ship; it is unable to fly or swim and may die

The populations of some sea animals, such as shrimp and red snapper, have become greatly depleted as a result of **overfishing**, together with pollution and the loss of suitable habitats. If stocks of fish fall below a certain level, it is likely that they will die out completely over time.

The effects of industry are not just felt in the urban environment. Working practices also produce problems in the countryside. Farmers use **pesticides** to protect their crops. This increases food production but at a cost to the environment.

FIG 4.11 Some insecticides are indiscriminate and will kill all insects whether they damage the crops or not

Activity 4.3

The drama of human activity

You should work in a small group for this activity. You will not need any equipment or materials but you will have to improvise by finding objects to support your role-play.

Here is what you should do:

1. Choose one of the effects industry has on the environment that were described in the lesson, or choose another you know about.

2. Write a short drama about the consequences this will have on the environment in the long-term if action is not taken now.

3. Your drama should be about three minutes long. Be prepared to act it out for the rest of the class.

Check your understanding

1. In order to conserve the environment, people must look for ways of sharing with other organisms and ways of minimising the impact of their activities on other organisms. Discuss how the provision of parks and lakes within towns might help to achieve this.

Fun fact

Water pollution is widespread in Trinidad and Tobago. Much of this is the result of industry. Industrial sources of water pollution include: wash from quarries, factory waste, overuse of chemicals such as fertilisers and pesticides, and waste oil.

Key terms

industry factories and other places where goods are processed or produced

atmospheric pollution pollution of the atmosphere by waste gases produced by industry and vehicles

overfishing removing more fish from the sea than can be replaced by natural breeding

pesticides chemicals used to control pests such as insects on crops

Genetically modified (GM) crops

We are learning how to:

- explain the impact of human activities on the local and global environment
- evaluate the issues surrounding genetically modified crops.

Genetically modified (GM) crops »

The nucleus of a cell contains information that will allow the cell to copy itself.

This information is found on tiny ribbon-like structures called **chromosomes**. Each chromosome contains many **genes**. Each gene is responsible for some feature of the organism it comes from. For example, your chromosomes contain genes that determine such things as the colour of your eyes.

Scientists can take the gene for a particular feature of one organism and insert it into the chromosomes of another. This is called **genetic engineering**. The technique is used to alter the characteristics of food crops, producing **genetically modified (GM) crops**.

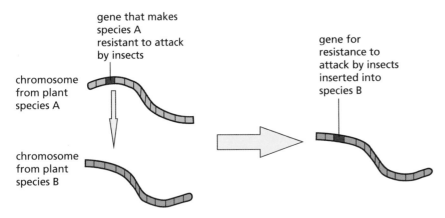

FIG 4.12 Genetic engineering

By modifying the genes of a food crop it may be possible to do things like:

- make the crop more resistant to disease
- make the crop more resistant to drought
- increase the yield of the crop.

Some scientists have concerns about GM crops. They say that GM crops could:

- alter the flavour of the food made from them
- cross-pollinate with wild species

FIG 4.13 Genetically modified maize

- lead to the development of superweeds or superpests that are not killed by herbicides and pesticides
- cause health problems for the organisms that eat them.

Activity 4.4

Debate on GM foods

You should work in a group for this activity. You will not need any equipment or materials.
Here is what you should do:

FIG 4.14 Genetically modified rice

Scientists have added a gene to wild rice to make a strain of rice that produces a substance called beta carotene. Beta carotene gives the wild rice a golden colour. It is needed by humans in order to make vitamin A.

Using whatever resource material is available, find out more about GM rice. Discuss in your group the possible advantages and disadvantages of this GM crop.

Check your understanding

1. State whether each of the following is a potential advantage or a disadvantage of GM crops.

   a) The yield of crops will increase.

   b) The taste of the modified crop will not be as good as the natural crop.

   c) The cost of buying food will be less.

   d) Crops can be grown more widely in places that are colder or have less rain.

   e) People might develop new allergies to a modified crop.

Key terms

chromosomes tiny ribbon-like structures containing information that enables a cell to make an exact copy of itself

genes parts of a chromosome that are responsible for the specific features of the organism they come from

genetic engineering taking the gene for a particular feature of one organism and inserting it into the chromosomes of another

genetically modified (GM) crop crop produced by using genetic engineering to modify its characteristics

Invasive alien species (IAS)

We are learning how to:

- explain the impact of human activities on the local and global environment
- become aware of the potential environmental problems that may arise by introducing animals and/or plants to a new environment.

Invasive alien species (IAS) 〉〉〉

Sometimes species from one area of the world are introduced into another. This might be by accident, such as insects arriving with imported goods, or it might be deliberate, such as the introduction of a new food crop.

Invasive alien species (IAS) are species that have out-competed native species and have spread throughout their new environment.

One major contributor to the success of an introduced species is a lack of natural **predators**. The populations of many species are controlled by predators, which eat them. Where there is no natural predator, the population of a species increases unchecked.

FIG 4.15 The pink mealy bug is native to southern Asia and arrived in Trinidad and Tobago in the 1990s

The pink mealy bug is a serious pest to agriculture because it attacks important crops.

The black wattle acacia tree produces lots of seeds. The species is out-competing native forest species for resources.

FIG 4.16 The black wattle acacia tree, which is native to Australia, was deliberately brought to Trinidad and Tobago in 1982 for forestry purposes

The red palm mite is so small it can be carried on the wind. It attacks coconut and other palms such as bananas.

The Asian green mussel has spread from Asia to other parts of the world in the ballast water of ships.

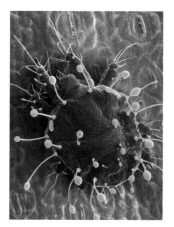

FIG 4.17 The red palm mite was first detected in Trinidad and Tobago in 2008

FIG 4.18 The Asian green mussel is well-established around the coasts of Trinidad and Tobago, where it has taken over the resources needed by native shellfish

Activity 4.5

The coconut moth

Here is what you need:

- internet and/or other resources.

Here is what you should do:

Find out what you can about the coconut moth. For example:

FIG 4.19 The coconut moth is another IAS found in Trinidad and Tobago

1. From where did it come to Trinidad and Tobago?

2. When was the coconut moth first observed in our country?

3. Why is it considered a pest?

Check your understanding

1. **a)** Suggest three ways in which an alien species might accidently come into a country. Give an example of the sort of organism involved.

   b) Suggest why countries have very strict rules about people importing animals and plants from abroad.

Fun fact

The introduction of a new species into a country is not always a bad thing. For example, sugar cane is not native to the Caribbean but it grows here well and causes few problems for indigenous species. The type of sugar cane grown all around the world is thought to have originally come from India.

Key terms

invasive alien species (IAS) species that have out-competed native species and have spread throughout their new environment

predators species that eat other species

Nature reserves

We are learning how to:

- explain the impact of human activities on the local and global environment
- understand the role of nature reserves in maintaining the environment.

Nature reserves »»

A **nature reserve** is an area of land that is protected and managed in order to preserve the various **habitats** it contains. It provides protection for the plants and animals that are found there.

Nature reserves often contain plants and animals that are **rare** or **endangered** and are therefore seldom observed elsewhere.

Trinidad and Tobago is blessed with many protected areas in the form of **national parks**, sanctuaries and reserves.

There are over 200 species of tree and liana in the Matura National Park. The park provides a home for endangered species such as the pawi and the ocelot.

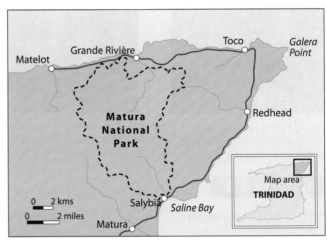

FIG 4.20 The Matura National Park is located in the north west of Trinidad and covers 9000 hectares, of which around 90 per cent is undisturbed forest

The Main Ridge Forest Reserve contains many different types of plant. It is also home to many species of animal, including the ocellated gecko.

FIG 4.22 The Main Ridge Forest Reserve is effectively the backbone of Tobago and consists of around 4000 hectares of highland and lowland tropical rainforest

FIG 4.21 The ocellated gecko can be found in the Main Ridge Forest Reserve

FIG 4.23 The Nariva Swamp is the largest freshwater wetland in Trinidad and Tobago

Fun fact

The Caroni Swamp, just south of Port of Spain, is the largest mangrove wetland in Trinidad. It is home to many kinds of bird, including the scarlet ibis.

During the day the scarlet ibis feed in Venezuela but at dusk they fly back across the sea to roost in the swamp.

The Nariva Swamp is on the east coast of Trinidad and covers an area of 6200 hectares.

The swamp contains four wetland vegetation types or **ecosystems**: mangrove swamp forest, palm forest, swamp wood and freshwater marsh. It is the home of many animal species including the West Indian manatee, white-fronted capuchin monkeys and numerous species of parrot and other birds.

Activity 4.6

Nature reserves and national parks

All of the class should participate in this activity.

1. Where is the nearest nature reserve or national park to where you live?
2. Have you ever visited this nature reserve?
3. Share your experiences with the class.

Check your understanding

1. **a)** Suggest some benefits plants and animals derive from nature reserves.
   b) Suggest some benefits people derive from nature reserves.

Key terms

nature reserve area of land that is protected and managed in order to preserve the various habitats it contains

habitats places where species live

rare low numbers in a population

endangered species in danger of extinction

national parks areas protected from development and other damaging human activities

ecosystems ways in which species live together

Deforestation

We are learning how to:

- explain the impact of human activities on the local and global environment
- evaluate the impact of deforestation.

Deforestation >>>

FIG 4.24 In 1498, most of Trinidad and Tobago was covered in forest – now only around 44 per cent of the islands are forested

Deforestation has occurred in Trinidad and Tobago, just as it has in other areas of the world. Scientists estimate that 80 000 square kilometres of forest are lost from the world each year.

Forest was cleared in Trinidad to allow sugar to be grown. In Brazil, large areas of rainforest are being cleared to create cattle ranches. Wood is an important commodity used for building lots of things. Another reason why forests are cleared is to sell the wood obtained from the trees.

Biodiversity is a measure of how many different species of plant are found in an area. Forests generally show a high biodiversity because there are a number of different habitats suitable for different plants and animals.

FIG 4.25 One reason that people cut down forests is to clear the land to grow crops or raise cattle

Fun fact

About 6.2 per cent or 14 000 hectares of the forested area of Trinidad and Tobago is primary forest. This type of forest has the highest amount of biodiversity.

Cutting down trees does not just affect the plants and animals that live in and on them; it also affects those that live on the forest floor. Plants that can only live in shade are exposed to the strong sunlight when the trees are removed. When these plants die, they no longer provide cover for the animals that live around them so the animals are also lost.

FIG 4.26 Without the protection of plant cover and the roots to hold the particles together, fertile topsoil dries out and is easily eroded by wind and heavy rainfall; the lower layers of soil that remain have few nutrients so very little grows in it

Deforestation can also lead to other undesirable environmental effects. It increases the likelihood of soil erosion during heavy rains. Burning the trees that have been cut down raises carbon dioxide levels in the air, and many more species of plants and animals are lost.

Activity 4.7

Conservation or exploitation?

You should work as a class on this activity. You will not need any equipment or materials.
Here is what you should do:

1. Carry out research into deforestation. Use the information you obtain to take part in a classroom debate on forests.

2. You must decide whether forests should be conserved at all costs or whether the forests should be exploited to provide for the needs of the people.

Key terms

deforestation cutting down trees in forests to clear land for other uses

biodiversity a measure of how many different species of plant are found in an area

Check your understanding

These satellite images show deforestation spreading in the Amazon rainforest around Rondonia in Brazil. The images were taken by satellite in 1975, 1992 and 2001.

1. **a)** How has the appearance of the area changed?

   b) Suggest why the changes have taken place.

   c) Suggest how the biodiversity of the area has changed, if at all, between 1975 and 2001.

   d) What effects of the changes might you expect to see if you had observed the land more closely in 2001?

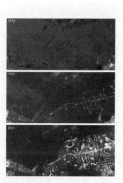

FIG 4.27

Biodiversity

We are learning how to:

- explain the impact of human activities on the local and global environment
- appreciate the impact of environmental issues on biodiversity.

Biodiversity »

Trinidad and Tobago has a wealth of ecosystems. It has the highest level of biodiversity in the Caribbean. The biodiversity of animals includes around: 420 species of bird, 600 species of butterfly, 95 species of mammal, 85 species of reptile, 30 species of amphibian and 54 species of freshwater fish.

In addition, there are thought to be around 2100 species of flowering plant. About 400 of these are native to Trinidad and Tobago.

FIG 4.28 The plant *Dicliptera aripoensis* is a native plant found only in the Heights of Aripo in Trinidad's Northern Range

FIG 4.29 Black-throated mango hummingbird (*Anthracothorax nigricollis*)

FIG 4.30 Scarlet peacock butterfly (*Anartia amathea*)

FIG 4.31 Malachite butterfly (*Siproea stelenes*)

FIG 4.32 Common iguana

The importance of biodiversity was highlighted in 2013 by governmental approval of the first National Wildlife Policy for Trinidad and Tobago. This recognises the importance of wildlife to the country.

Since organisms are suited to particular habitats, it follows that ecosystems that offer the largest variety of habitats will attract the most species of organism. Anything that alters an ecosystem by reducing the variety of habitats will reduce biodiversity.

Urbanisation, industry and deforestation greatly reduce biodiversity. However, even small-scale changes in land usage can have a significant effect.

FIG 4.33 **a)** The fields are small, separated by hedges, and each contains a different crop; species of wild plant grow in the hedges

b) The field is large and contains only one crop (**monoculture**) so there is much less hedge and far fewer wild plants

A diversity of plants will attract lots of different insects and other animals. The method of cultivation in Fig 4.33a) therefore will support a much greater biodiversity than that in Fig 4.33b).

Activity 4.8

United Nations Decade on Diversity

You should work in a small group on this activity.

The years 2011 to 2020 are the United Nations Decade of Diversity. Use the internet and any other resources you have to find out more about the aims of the Decade of Diversity and how it is hoped these aims will be achieved. Explain how you could contribute to achieving these aims.

Check your understanding

1.

FIG 4.34 **a)** A conifer forest in which only one type of tree grows
b) A mixed forest in which many different types of tree are found

Which forest is likely to show the higher level of biodiversity? Explain your answer.

Fun fact

The golden tree frog *Phyllodytes auratus* is found only on El Tucuche in the Northern Range. It is not found anywhere else in the world. There are other species of flora and fauna indigenous to Trinidad and Tobago.

Species of flora and fauna (especially fish) north of the Northern Range in Trinidad are different from those south of the Northern Range.

Key term

monoculture using land to grow only one crop in a large field

Threatened species in Trinidad and Tobago

We are learning how to:

- explain the impact of human activities on the local and global environment
- identify local species of animal and plant that are in danger of extinction.

Threatened species in Trinidad and Tobago ≫

Pawi

FIG 4.35 The pawi is a medium-sized bird that lives in forests and is the only bird that is found exclusively on the island of Trinidad

The pawi is at risk of extinction because of hunting and loss of habitat. It is now only found in an area of 150 km² of forest in the north east of Trinidad.

Ocelot

Ocelots live alone and hunt at night. The ocelot is not threatened with extinction worldwide as it is found in some other countries. However, the population of ocelots in Trinidad is falling due to hunting and loss of habitat.

FIG 4.36 Trinidad is the only part of the Caribbean where the ocelot is found, and the ocelot is the only wild cat present on the island

West Indian manatee

FIG 4.37 The West Indian manatee is a large aquatic creature that feeds on vegetation and is found in the waters surrounding some Caribbean and American countries

The manatee has no natural enemies but is under threat due to the activities of people.

These include collision with boats, ingestion of fish hooks and litter, and entanglement in fishing nets.

Trinidad white-fronted capuchin monkey

At the last census of these monkeys, in 2008, the estimated total population of this monkey was only 61. The number is small due mainly to a loss of habitat.

FIG 4.38 White-fronted capuchin monkeys are found in a number of countries in South America, but the Trinidad white-fronted capuchin monkey is a sub-species found only in the rainforests of Trinidad

Activity 4.9

Taking action to help a threatened species

You should work in a small group for this activity. You will not need any equipment or materials.

Here is what you should do:

One of the ways of helping a threatened species is to make the public more aware of their plight. This might encourage people to do things like:

- write to the government suggesting that action should be taken

- donate money to fund conservation

- take more care when walking or driving in the countryside.

Choose one of the animals described in the lesson and plan a campaign to make people more aware of its plight. Your campaign could include things like:

- writing an article for the local newspaper

- designing a poster to be placed somewhere prominent

- designing leaflets that can be distributed.

Check your understanding

1. Using available resources, find out more about the white-tailed sabrewing hummingbird and why it is threatened.

Fun fact

The International Union for Conservation of Nature places threatened plants and animals into three categories.

- Vulnerable species have a high risk of becoming extinct in the wild in the medium-term future.

- Endangered species have a very high risk of becoming extinct in the wild in the near future.

- Critically endangered species have an extremely high risk of becoming extinct in the wild in the immediate future.

Global warming

We are learning how to:

- explain the impact of human activities on the local and global environment
- consider the possible effects of global warming.

Global warming 》》

The average surface temperature of the Earth has increased by about 0.8 °C over the last 100 years. Much of this increase has occurred in the last 30 years. This suggests that the trend in rising temperature is increasing.

This may not sound like much of an increase, but even this small rise has caused major changes to the climate in different parts of the world. This is known as **global warming**.

FIG 4.39 The North Pole is at the extreme top of the Earth and is a very cold place, even in the summer

The average winter temperature at the North Pole is around −34 °C while in the summer the average is around 0 °C. Scientists who study the North Pole have been aware for some time that average temperatures are increasing. The northern polar ice cap is slowly getting smaller and the ice is getting thinner as more ice turns to water.

In some parts of the world the summers are getting much hotter and drier. Warmer weather has led to water shortages and **droughts** in certain parts of the world.

Water is being used up more quickly than it can be replaced by nature.

FIG 4.40 The level of water in reservoirs is lower than it has been in the past because of increased evaporation and lack of rain

In areas of the world where there are large forests, the vegetation is much drier than in the past due to higher temperatures and lack of rain.

FIG 4.41 Dry vegetation catches fire very easily and forest fires have destroyed huge areas of forest

Activity 4.10

The effects of drought

You should work in a small group for this activity.

Here is what you should do:

1. Discuss what effects a drought is likely to have on people and on wildlife.

2. Imagine there is a drought in your area now. Discuss what steps you could take to reduce the use of water.

Check your understanding

1. Copy and complete the following sentences by writing either 'increasing' or 'decreasing'.

   a) The surface temperature of the Earth has been _____ over the last 100 years.

   b) The thickness of the ice at the North Pole is _____ .

   c) In some parts of the world summers are getting hotter and drier. The effects of this are that:

      i)   water levels in lakes and reservoirs are _____ .

      ii) the risk of forest fires is _____ .

      iii) the number of wild animals and farm animals dying from lack of food and water is _____ .

Fun fact

There is land beneath the ice at the South Pole, but the North Pole consists entirely of ice. If the northern polar ice cap were to completely melt it would be possible to sail over the North Pole.

Key terms

global warming rise in average surface temperature of the Earth

droughts lack of rain

The greenhouse effect

We are learning how to:

- explain the impact of human activities on the local and global environment
- explain the greenhouse effect.

The greenhouse effect 》》》

Greenhouse gases are gases that can absorb and emit heat radiation. The main greenhouse gases in the **atmosphere**, as far as global warming is concerned, are water vapour, carbon dioxide, methane and ozone.

Many scientists believe that global warming is caused by increasing concentrations of greenhouse gases in the atmosphere. This increase is the result of human activities.

The increase in concentrations of greenhouse gases in the atmosphere is commonly called the **greenhouse effect** because the greenhouse gases in the atmosphere have a similar effect to the glass roof and sides of a greenhouse. Heat becomes trapped in the greenhouse causing the temperature to rise.

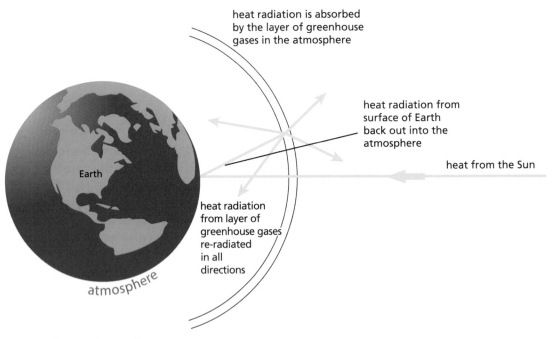

FIG 4.42 The greenhouse effect

The greenhouse effect should more correctly be called the enhanced greenhouse effect. The greenhouse effect has existed as long as the Earth has had an atmosphere. Without the greenhouse effect, Earth would never have become warm enough to support life as we know it.

The problem is that the concentrations of the greenhouse gases have increased significantly over the past two hundred years. Now, too much heat is being trapped on the Earth by the greenhouse gases and not enough is escaping into space.

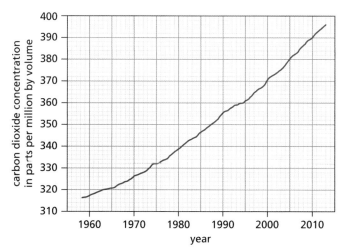

FIG 4.43 Global warming coincides with a slow but steady rise in the concentration of carbon dioxide in the atmosphere, which provides evidence of the link between global warming and the effect of increasing concentrations of greenhouse gases

Activity 4.11

Tackling global warming

You should work in a small group for this activity.

Here is what you need:

- plain paper
- coloured pencils or paints.

Here is what you should do:

Global warming is a global problem but that does not mean individuals cannot take action to reduce it.

1. What action can you take as an individual to reduce global warming?

2. Design a leaflet informing people about the problems of global warming and what they can do to help reduce it.

Check your understanding

1. State whether each of the following increase or decrease the concentration of carbon dioxide in the air.

   a) Burning fossil fuels like coal and natural gas
   b) Photosynthesis
   c) Road vehicles that run on petrol and diesel
   d) Deforestation

Fun fact

Concentration is sometimes expressed as the number of parts per million. For example, the concentration of carbon dioxide is 396 parts per million.

This means that for every 1 000 000 particles in the air, 396 of them are carbon dioxide. We can also express this as a percentage:

$$\frac{396}{1\ 000\ 000} = \frac{0.0396}{100}$$

$$= 0.0396\%$$

Key terms

greenhouse gases gases that can absorb and emit heat radiation

atmosphere layer of gases above the surface of the Earth

greenhouse effect the increase in concentrations of greenhouse gases in the atmosphere

Biodegradable and non-biodegradable

We are learning how to:

- explain the impact of human activities on the local and global environment
- identify which materials are biodegradable and which are not.

Biodegradable and non-biodegradable ❯❯❯

Waste is not a good thing for a number of reasons.

- It is ugly and has an unpleasant smell.
- It is expensive to deal with.
- It may contain substances that damage the environment.
- It provides a breeding ground for pests such as flies.
- It often contains materials that can be recycled.

Some materials decompose when buried in the ground due to the action of **decomposer** organisms such as bacteria, fungi and worms. These materials are described as **biodegradable**.

Other materials are **non-biodegradable**. They can remain buried in the ground for many years and remain unchanged.

FIG 4.44 One method of disposing of waste is to bury it in the ground as what is called landfill – this landfill site is in Grenada

Activity 4.12

Finding out what happens when materials are buried in soil

You will need to do this activity outside.

Here is what you need:

- trowel or spade
- stale bread
- empty plastic bottle
- sticks to mark the holes.

Here is what you should do:

1. Dig two holes about 10 cm deep close to each other.
2. In one hole place a piece of stale bread.
3. In the second hole place an empty plastic bottle.
4. Pour some water on each material.
5. Fill the holes with soil.

Fun fact

Scientists are developing plastics that are biodegradable. They will be made from raw materials such as corn and potato starch. They will also be sustainable, unlike plastics made from crude oil, which are not sustainable as the oil they are made from will one day run out.

6. Place markers so that you can find where each material is buried again.

7. After around two weeks gently remove the soil from each hole.

8. Carefully examine the stale bread and the plastic bottle.

9. Describe what has happened, if anything, to the stale bread and to the plastic bottle.

If vegetable waste is left out in the open or dug into soil, it will eventually rot away.

Rotted waste from a compost heap provides nutrients for plants.

Plastics are useful but they have one big disadvantage. Plastic is not broken down by natural processes and is therefore non-biodegradable.

FIG 4.45 Vegetable waste can be described as biodegradable because it is degraded or broken down by biological processes

FIG 4.46 Waste plastic that has been dug into the soil will remain unchanged for tens and maybe even hundreds of years

In general, materials that are made from living things are biodegradable, while manmade materials are not.

Check your understanding

1. Which of these are biodegradable and which are not? Make two lists.

aluminium can	cardboard box	coffee grounds
glass jar	orange peel	paper bag
plastic tray	porcelain mug	stale bread
wooden skewer		

Key terms

waste material that humans throw away

decomposers organisms such as bacteria, fungi and worms that decompose organic waste

biodegradable materials that decompose when buried in the ground as a result of decomposers acting on them

non-biodegradable materials that do not decompose when buried in the ground

Reducing demand to reduce waste

We are learning how to:

- explain the impact of human activities on the local and global environment
- reduce demand in order to reduce waste.

Reducing demand in order to reduce waste »

To decide how best to deal with waste, we need to know what people throw away.

Activity 4.13

Analysing the contents of a bag of rubbish

For this activity you need to work in a group.

Here is what you need:

- pair of rubber gloves
- bag of rubbish
- new bin bag
- waste newspaper.

⚠️ **SAFETY**

The person handling the waste materials must wear rubber gloves.

Here is what you should do:

1. As a group, decide how you are going to divide up the waste. Aim for six categories, for example: metal, plastic, glass, waste food and peelings, paper and card, and other materials.

2. Spread newspaper over the top of your table to protect it.

3. Open a bin bag so it is ready to receive the waste.

4. Open the bag of rubbish and pour some of it onto the table.

5. Classify each item under one of your headings and then put it into the new bin bag.

6. Other members of the group should record each item in the correct category list.

To reduce the waste going to landfill or disposed of in other ways, we can do three things. We call these the 3Rs.

- **Reduce** – some of the things we use may not be necessary.

Fun fact

The use of plastic bags is banned in some countries such as Bangladesh and China.

- **Reuse** – some things can be reused or repaired rather than thrown away.

- **Recycle** – some things are made of materials that can be recycled.

People do not eat the skins of some fruits so why put them in bags? Reduce waste by reducing the amount of materials used.

Some products are sold in a concentrated form. Why do you think this is done?

FIG 4.47 Many foods are already in packets so they do not need to be put in bags

The average home receives lots of unwanted mail each year.

FIG 4.48 You use a small amount of a concentrated product each time so the product lasts longer and there are fewer empty containers

FIG 4.49 If the amount of junk mail and circulars was reduced this would mean less waste

Check your understanding

1. Bottled water is often available in different-sized bottles.

   a) How can buying your bottled water in the largest size available reduce the amount of waste you create?

   b) Suggest another advantage of buying large packs of products.

2. Environmentalists want the government to ban the use of plastic bags in Trinidad and Tobago. They argue that plastic bags cause all sorts of environmental problems. They maintain that there are alternatives to plastic bags that do just as good a job. Make a list of arguments for and against a ban on plastic bags.

Key terms

reduce some of the things we use that end up as waste may not be necessary

reuse some things can be reused or repaired rather than thrown away

recycle some things are made of materials that can be recycled

Reusing to reduce waste

We are learning how to:

- explain the impact of human activities on the local and global environment
- reuse in order to reduce waste.

Reusing to reduce waste ⟫⟫

People can reduce waste by using objects and materials more than once.

In some shops, goods are placed into disposable plastic bags. The bags are meant to be used once and thrown away. This is bad for the environment. The plastic used to make the bags is non-biodegradable and plastic bags are not easy to recycle.

FIG 4.50 A shopping bag can be used many times before it has to be thrown away; using a shopping bag reduces waste and is good for the environment

FIG 4.51 Using lunch boxes that can be taken home and washed each night is much better for the environment than taking food in plastic boxes and bags that are then thrown away; Styrotex containers are also used a lot

Why not refill a clean empty water bottle with your drink each day instead of having a drink in a disposable bottle?

FIG 4.52 Liquid soap dispensers do not need to be thrown away when they are empty; they can be refilled (one refill pack lasts a long time)

Activity 4.14

Encouraging people to reuse

You should work in a small group for this activity.

Here is what you need:

- coloured pencils or paints
- large sheet of sugar paper or card.

Here is what you should do:

1. Discuss how people might be encouraged to reuse things.

2. Design a poster informing people about how reusing can reduce the amount of waste they generate.

3. Sketch out your poster on paper.

4. When you are satisfied with it, redraw it on a large sheet of paper or card.

Check your understanding

1. Some printer ink cartridges are refillable.

   a) Suggest some advantages to having print cartridges that can be refilled.

   b) Is it possible to reuse an item for ever? Explain your answer.

> **Environmental fact**
>
> Research has shown that 80 per cent of the waste floating in the seas around Trinidad and Tobago is made of plastic. This works out at about 15 000 plastic items per square kilometre. Plastic is non-biodegradable so this situation is going to get worse.

Recycling to reduce waste

We are learning how to:

- explain the impact of human activities on the local and global environment
- recycle to reduce waste.

Recycling to reduce waste ›››

Recycling means using materials that are found in waste to make new things. It reduces:

- the amount of waste that has to be treated by burning or landfill
- the demand on natural resources
- the amount of energy needed to produce materials.

Materials that can be recycled include metals, glass, some plastics, paper and cardboard.

In some countries each household is given different bins that are used for the various types of waste. For example, a household might have a separate bin for:

- materials that can be recycled such as glass, metals, plastics and paper
- vegetable and garden waste that can be composted
- waste that cannot be recycled and is therefore incinerated or buried in the ground.

FIG 4.53 Many countries have recycle points where people can bring waste that can be recycled

Recycle points can be found in places like supermarket car parks. There is a large bin for each type of material for recycling.

Fun fact

The demand for metals such as aluminium increases every year. By 2020 it is estimated that 97 million tonnes of aluminium will be used each year and, of that, 31 million tonnes, almost one third, will come from recycled scrap. Recycling works and it has an important role to play in ensuring we do not run out of essential resources in the future.

Activity 4.15

Planning a recycle centre at your school

You should work in a small group for this activity. You will not need any equipment or materials.

Here is what you should do:

1. Discuss how you could encourage fellow students to recycle their waste.

2. Decide on a suitable position in your school to place a recycle bank.

3. What are your reasons for choosing this position?

4. Suppose your recycle bank is to have four recycle bins. What type of recyclable waste would you collect in each bin?

5. What would you do with the recycled waste you collect?

In addition to reducing waste, recycling may also save money and energy.

Recycling scrap aluminium such as from empty drink cans requires only five per cent of the energy used to make new aluminium from bauxite. Aluminium does not rot so it can be recycled many times. It is thought that three quarters of all of the aluminium produced in the USA over the last hundred years is still in use today.

FIG 4.54 Aluminium cans are melted down to form aluminium ingots

Check your understanding

1. Fig 4.56 shows some bins used for recycling.

FIG 4.56 Some bins used for recycling

a) What material is being recycled in these bins?
b) How is the material sorted?
c) What proportion of this material can be recycled?

FIG 4.55 Aluminium ingots are identical to the aluminium made from bauxite

Key term

recycle points places where people can bring waste that can be recycled

Improving the local environment

We are learning how to:

- explain the impact of human activities on the local and global environment
- improve the local environment.

Improving the local environment ≫

You might decide to improve a place near where you live, or it might be an area of your school compound. How can the area you have chosen be improved?

Litter is often a problem. Once people start to deposit litter in an area it acts like a magnet and, before long, the pile of litter grows. The only solution is to clear away the litter.

FIG 4.57 When litter is cleared, provide a litter bin and place signs to remind people that they should use it

The area will look much better without litter but it may not look very interesting. What makes an area more interesting are plants and shrubs, and the animals that visit them.

Here are some ideas to get you thinking about what you should plant.

- Flowers attract pollinating insects and hummingbirds.

- Trees and shrubs provide fruit and berries for animals.

- Ground cover provides places where small animals can hide.

FIG 4.58 Plants and shrubs

To get lots of biodiversity you need to provide as many different habitats as possible. You might:

- dig a small pond to provide a habitat for aquatic plants and animals, as well as a place where other animals will come to drink

- include a few pieces of old tree trunk so that organisms can feed off the decaying wood and fungi can grow

- build a bug hotel by placing lengths of hollow bamboo inside an old pipe.

Activity 4.16

Making somewhere better

You should work in a small group for this activity. You will not need any equipment or materials.

Here is what you should do:

1. Identify a small area either near where you live or in your school that you think could be improved.

2. Make a list of the things that you could do to improve this area. Look at examples from elsewhere to give you some ideas.

3. Make a list of the tools and materials that you would need.

4. Research the types of shrubs and plants that would be best suited to your project.

5. Decide how you would maintain your area. For example, litter bins do not empty themselves and plants and shrubs will need watering in the dry season.

Check your understanding

1.

FIG 4.59 In some cities, small parks are built between the buildings

Make a list of some of the advantages of having small parks in cities.

> **Fun fact**
>
> Some areas of towns and cities have community garden clubs organised by local residents.
>
> The people within a community all work together in order to improve their environment.

Review of Environmental impact of human activities

- Human activity has an impact on the environment. As the population of the world increases, the effect humans have on the environment increases.

- Urbanisation is the increase in the proportion of people in a country who live in towns and cities. Urbanisation is increasing in many countries as people come to towns looking for work or for other reasons. As towns and cities grow larger, so does their impact on the environment.

- As a country develops, its industry grows larger. Industry has an impact on the environment due to increased use of land for buildings and roads, and the creation of various types of pollution.

- Genetically modified (GM) crops are food crops that have been modified by adding favourable genes. This might:
  - increase the yield
  - reduce the time until the crop is ready to harvest
  - make the crop resistant to attack by insects
  - make the crop resistant to drought.

- GM crops appear to be the answer to world food shortages but some scientists believe that they may cause damage to the environment in different ways.

- Invasive alien species (IAS) are species of organism that have been transferred from one area of the world to another, either accidentally or deliberately. Where an organism has an abundance of food and no natural enemies, its population rapidly increases at the expense of native species. IAS may also carry diseases that can be transferred to native organisms. Examples of IAS in Trinidad and Tobago include the pink mealy bug, the black wattle acacia tree, the red palm mite, the Asian green mussel and the coconut moth.

- Nature reserves are areas where human activity is strictly controlled. This allows the organisms that are found there to live in the absence of human activities, which increases their chances of flourishing. Reserves also provide a haven where people can observe and study wildlife. There are a number of nature reserves in Trinidad and Tobago.

- Deforestation is the removal of trees so that land can be used for building or for farming. The removal of trees destroys many different habitats, both in the trees and on the ground beneath them. The results of deforestation are the loss of many species of organism from an area and an increase in soil erosion.

- Biodiversity is the number of different species of organism found in an area. Biodiversity is high when an area has many different habitats. Trinidad and Tobago has the highest level of biodiversity in the whole of the Caribbean.

- Urbanisation, industry and deforestation all reduce the level of biodiversity in an area. Other human activities, such as changes in land usage, also impact on biodiversity.

- Loss of habitat can leave some species of plants and animals threatened and in danger of becoming extinct. Examples of threatened species in Trinidad and Tobago include the pawi, the ocelot, the West Indian manatee, the Trinidad white-fronted capuchin monkey and the white-tailed sabrewing hummingbird.

- Global warming is the result of a small but significant increase in the average temperature of the Earth. It is thought to be responsible for such things as changes in weather patterns around the world, the melting of the polar ice caps, an increase in forest fires and droughts.

- Global warming is thought to be the result of the greenhouse effect. Some gases, including carbon dioxide, are described as greenhouse gases because, in the atmosphere, they trap heat radiation from the Earth and prevent it from passing out into space. Over the past 200 years the concentration of carbon dioxide in the atmosphere has slowly risen due to activities like the large-scale burning of fossil fuels.

- Materials can be classified as biodegradable or non-biodegradable on the basis of whether or not they rot in the ground. Natural materials are generally biodegradable while synthetic materials, such as glass and plastic, are not. Large amounts of non-biodegradable waste are a serious threat to the environment.

- People can reduce the amount of waste they create by:
  - reducing the amount of materials they use
  - reusing things until they are worn out
  - recycling materials to make new things.

- A local environment can be improved in a number of ways including:
  - removing litter and waste materials
  - providing a litter bin
  - planting shrubs and plants that will attract insects, birds and other animals
  - providing a source of water
  - creating lots of different habitats.

Review questions on Environmental impact of human activities

1. **a)** What is meant by the term 'biodegradable'?
   b) Give three examples of materials that are:
     i) biodegradable
     ii) non-biodegradable.
   c) Why is non-biodegradable waste a threat to the environment?

2. Copy and complete the following sentences.
   a) Biodiversity is a measure of the number of different types of _____ and
       _____ .
   b) Matura National Park is in the _____ of Trinidad.
   c) In a national park human activities are _____ .
   d) In a national park the level of _____ is high because organisms are protected.
   e) One of the rare _____ living in the Matura National Park is the ocelot.

3. Copy and complete the following sentences using words from the box.

endangered   extinct   habitats   protected

   a) When land is cleared for farms natural _____ are destroyed.
   b) When populations of plants and animals fall they are said to be _____ .
   c) If something is not done to conserve plants and animals they may become
       _____ .
   d) In national parks, plants and animals are _____ from the activities of people.

4. Describe ways in which building and operating a sugar factory might harm the local environment.

5. The pawi is a bird that lives in the canopy of hill forests in Trinidad and Tobago. It feeds on fruit from the trees and builds its nest high up in them.

   a) The pawi is classified as an environmentally sensitive species in Trinidad and Tobago. What do you think this means?
   b) Suggest some reasons why any loss of forest would be detrimental to the population of pawi.

6. Scientists have developed a genetically modified corn that produces a poison that kills harmful insects. Decide whether each of the following is an advantage or a disadvantage of growing this crop.

   a) The farmer no longer has to buy insecticides.

b) If insects are exposed to the poison continually, new strains might develop that are immune to it.

c) The poison produced by the corn may act on other insects that are not pests.

d) The farmer no longer has to spray insecticides over the crop and the surrounding environment.

e) Poison eaten by insects might enter a food chain.

f) Yields of corn will increase.

7. Here is a short extract from a newspaper article about soya beans.

   Farmers who grow soya beans have been suffering from reduced yields for a long time. The problem is competition from weeds in their fields. A new genetically engineered variety of soya bean may be the answer to their problem. This new variety of soya bean can withstand glyphosphate, a herbicide that kills other plants.

   Use this information to help you answer the following questions.

   a) What would be the result of spraying a field containing the new type of soya beans and weeds?

   b) What would be the benefit to the farmer of growing the new type of soya beans? Explain your answer.

   c) Sometimes crop plants can interbreed with weeds. Suggest one problem that might arise if the new type of soya beans did this.

8. Some rabbits were accidently introduced to an island upon which there were no natural predators. Fig 4.60 shows how the population of rabbits increased over a period of years.

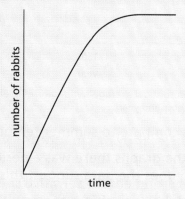

FIG 4.60 Graph to show rabbit population over time

   a) What name is given to a species that, when introduced to an area, increases its numbers very quickly?

   b) Suggest why the number of rabbits reached a constant value even though there were no natural predators on the island.

c) Rabbits eat green plants. What effect would the introduction of rabbits to the island have on:

    i) the plant population?

    ii) the populations of other animals that eat plants?

d) What effect would introducing the rabbits have on the level of biodiversity on the island? Explain your answer.

9. The graphs in Fig 4.61 show how the average summer and winter temperatures in Western Europe have changed over the past thousand years.

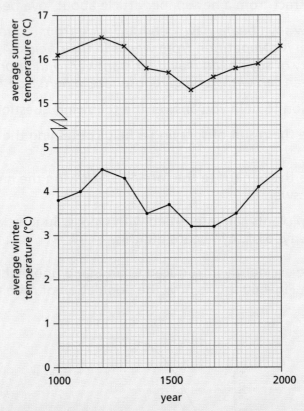

FIG 4.61 Graph to show average temperatures in Europe over the last thousand years

a) How do winter temperatures compare to summer temperatures?

b) During the period shown in the graphs there was a period of 100 years that people call the 'Little Ice Age'. When does the data suggest this was?

c) Some scientists believe that global warming is the result of natural fluctuations in the Earth's climate. What period over the past thousand years would support this view and why?

10. Mayfly nymphs live in fast-flowing streams. They need lots of oxygen dissolved in the water. A factory uses water from a stream as a coolant. The water returned to the stream is clean but is warmer by several degrees.

A student carried out a survey in which she counted the number of mayfly nymphs at different distances from the place where the water is returned from the factory. The table shows her results.

Distance from where water returned from the factory (metres)	10	20	30	40	50	60
Number of mayfly nymphs	0	4	7	11	19	18

TABLE 4.1 Mayfly numbers near a factory outlet

a) In what way does the factory pollute the stream?

b) What do the results indicate about how the solubility of oxygen in the water changes with temperature? Explain your answer.

c) Estimate the distance at which the water in the stream returns to its normal temperature.

Improving your local environment

Are there things about your local environment you think somebody should do something about? Maybe that somebody is you?

People are often appalled by rubbish dumped in their community but they don't know what to do about it. As a scientist you have analytical skills that can help your community.

Rubbish doesn't appear on our streets by magic. It appears because people are careless or sometimes just lazy. You are going to do what you can to improve the situation in your community.

FIG 4.62 Litter is unsightly and dangerous

1. You are going to work in a group of 3 or 4 to reduce rubbish in your community. It would be best if all of the students in your group live near one another. The tasks are:

   • to identify the areas of your community which are affected by rubbish
   • to analyse the rubbish to see what you are dealing with
   • to try and identify sources of this rubbish
   • to find out what help is available from local authorities
   • to take steps to reduce or even eliminate the rubbish on the streets of your community.

a) Before you can tackle the problem of rubbish on the streets of your community you need to identify the problem areas. It's possible that there is rubbish all over the place but are there particular areas which are always heavily littered? For example, are there always lots of sweet wrappers in the area around the local sweet shop? You might:

   ○ draw a simple map of the area around your community
   ○ grade areas from 1 (seldom much rubbish) to 5 (badly affected most of the time).

b) As well as where, you also need to know what and how much. You might:

   • gather the rubbish from a sample area and analyse it. You might separate it into categories like: paper and cardboard, plastic, glass, etc.

FIG 4.63 Quantifying the problem

- weigh the amount of rubbish you gather by putting it in a bin liner and using a spring balance, this will give you some quantitative data
- use your sampling to estimate the size of the problem for the whole area around your community.

c) Now is the time to do some detective work. Is it possible to deduce where the rubbish has come from? For example you might consider:

- Is there a fast food outlet in your community that has distinctive packaging?
- Is there a garage in your community that provides distinctive plastic gloves or paper towels to customers?
- Is there a supermarket with the name on their plastic bags?

FIG 4.64 Fast food packaging

Try and identify the sources of as much of the rubbish as you can and quantify the amount from each source that is currently lying around on the streets.

d) Find out whether the local authorities have a legal obligation to deal with rubbish in your community. It may be that they have but unless somebody contacts them they don't know about it. Find out what the procedures are for requesting help with rubbish. Is there a telephone help line?

e) Now you need to think about contacting those people in charge of those places that you consider the sources of a significant amount of the rubbish. Before you write consider the following:
- if you start by accusing people of being responsible for littering the streets of your community they are likely to go on the defensive and you will get very little help from them
- if you explain to people what you are doing, give a brief account of what you have found and invite them to help find a solution to the problem they are far more likely to respond favourably.

f) If you are invited to discuss the problems of litter with someone make sure you are well prepared. You should be able to give a clear account of what you have found and if a person says, 'How can I help you?', you should be able to respond with some ideas of how things can be improved.

g) Prepare an oral report on what you have done. Take photographs during the different stages of the activity which can be used to illustrate your report. Some pictures of 'before' and 'after' might give your audience some idea of how successful you were.

Unit 5: Electricity

Conductors and insulators

Electricity is a very common and very convenient form of energy. We can send it from one place to another along wires.

Insulators are substances that do not conduct electricity.

We connect appliances safely into an electricity supply using plugs and sockets.

Circuits

FIG 5.1 The metal wire is a conductor and conducts electricity, but around it there is a plastic sheath that is an insulator

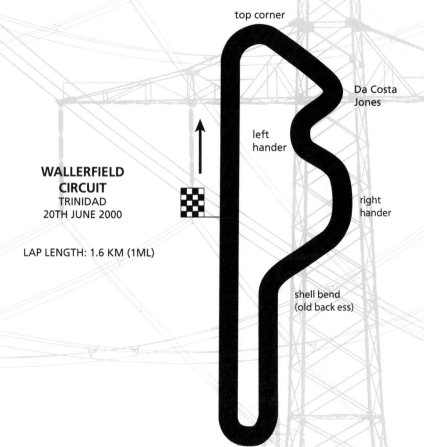

top corner

Da Costa Jones

left hander

right hander

WALLERFIELD CIRCUIT
TRINIDAD
20TH JUNE 2000

LAP LENGTH: 1.6 KM (1ML)

shell bend
(old back ess)

hairpin

FIG 5.2 A circuit, like at Wallerfield International Raceway, is a complete pathway that things can go around

FIG 5.3 Cars race round the Wallerfield circu

We can provide a complete pathway or circuit to allow electricity to flow.

Current

An electric current passes around a circuit. We measure current using an ammeter.

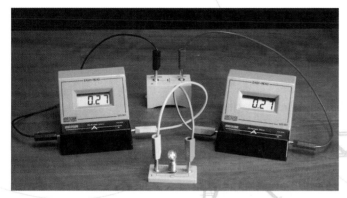

FIG 5.4 When an ammeter is placed in a circuit with a battery and a lamp it measures the amount of current that flows; the current is the same on both sides of the lamp

Circuit diagrams

Electrical components can be difficult and time-consuming to draw. Scientists use symbols of electrical components instead.

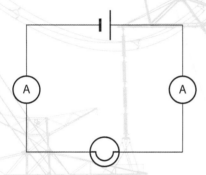

FIG 5.5 Scientists use circuit diagrams to show how the components in a circuit are connected together – each component has its own symbol

Can you guess which component in Fig 5.4 is represented by each of the symbols in Fig 5.5? Check the symbols shown on page 96 to see if you are correct.

Series and parallel

The components of electrical circuits can be placed both in series and in parallel. Connecting components in different ways affects their properties.

> ### Something to think about
>
> Long before people knew anything about electricity, people were aware that certain fish were capable of giving 'electric' shocks.
>
> As early as 2750 BC, Ancient Egyptians were referring to the Nile electric catfish as the 'Thunderer of the Nile' and believed it protected the other fish in the river.
>
> The Ancient Greeks knew that the numbing effect of the shock travelled along some materials (conductors) but not others (insulators).

FIG 5.6 a) In a single string of pearls, the pearls are placed in series, one after another b) When several strings of pearls are placed together, the strings run parallel with each other

Conductors and insulators

We are learning how to:

- distinguish between electrical insulators and conductors
- relate flow of current to conduction.

Conductors and insulators »

Electricity is a form of energy. It can pass easily through some materials but not others.

- Materials that allow an electric current to flow through them are called electrical **conductors**.

- Materials that prevent the flow of an electric current are called electrical **insulators**.

Activity 5.1

Conductors and insulators

Here is what you will need:

- battery of three cells
- lamp
- two crocodile clips
- connecting wires
- samples of materials, e.g. aluminium, copper, plastic, rubber, wood.

Here is what you should do:

1. Connect the components of the circuit together as shown in Fig 5.7.

2. Before testing the sample materials, test the circuit by touching the crocodile clips together. If the circuit is complete the lamp should light up. If the lamp does not light up, check all the connections.

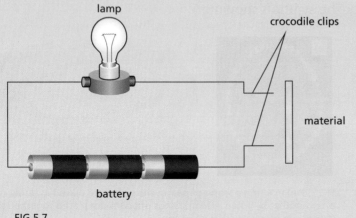

FIG 5.7

3. Take the first sample of material and clip the crocodile clips to each end of it. If the lamp lights the material is a conductor. If the bulb does not light the material is an insulator.

4. Present your observations in the form of a table. On one side write the names of the conducting materials, and on the other write the names of the insulating materials.

Metallic structure

Metals are all excellent conductors of electricity. To understand why, we need to consider **metallic structure**. Metals consist of a matrix of particles surrounded by a 'sea' of negatively charged **electrons**. These electrons are delocalised and free to move about.

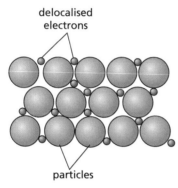

delocalised electrons

particles

FIG 5.8 Structure of a metal

When a conductor, such as a metal wire, is connected to a battery, electrons flow through the conductor carrying electrical charge. Electricity is a flow of electrons.

Insulators, such as plastics and glass, do not have delocalised electrons so they are unable to conduct electricity.

Check your understanding

1. Arrange the following materials into two lists: conductors and insulators.

| aluminium | copper | glass | iron |
| plastic | rubber | steel | wood |

Fun fact

The best conductor is the metal silver, followed by copper, then gold and then aluminium. Why are electric wires made of copper and not silver?

Key terms

conductors materials that allow an electric current to flow through them

insulators materials that prevent the flow of an electric current

metallic structure a matrix of particles surrounded by a 'sea' of negatively charged electrons

electrons negatively charged particles

Electricity and safety

We are learning how to:

- distinguish between electrical insulators and conductors
- use electricity safely.

Electricity and safety ⟫

Electricity is potentially dangerous so we must learn how to use it safely.

Some plugs have two pins and some have three. Sockets may have caps to prevent children poking things into them.

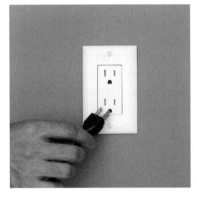 

FIG 5.9 An electrical appliance is connected to the mains electricity supply by a plug, which fits into a socket

Activity 5.2

Examining a plug and socket

Here is what you need:

- plug
- socket.

 SAFETY
Even though plugs and sockets are made of plastic, they should never be touched with wet hands. There is a danger that wetness will pass into the plug or socket and this can result in an electric shock.

Here is what you should do:

1. Look carefully at the plug and observe where the wires from the appliance will be connected.
2. Notice that when the plug is placed fully in the socket there are no exposed metal parts.
3. Look carefully at the socket and where the wires from the supply will be connected.
4. Notice that the holes for the pins of the plug are very small, which prevents people accidentally pushing something into the holes.
5. Notice also that the plug pins must be fully into the socket before they connect with the electricity supply. This means that no parts of the plug pins are exposed.
6. From what type of material are the bodies of the plug and socket made?

Two wires are needed to make a circuit. Some plugs have three pins and three wires. The third wire is called the **earth wire**. It protects the user should a fault develop in the appliance.

If the wires in a metal table lamp came loose and touched the metal body, anyone touching it would receive an electric shock. The earth wire is connected to the metal body. Most of the current will pass through it so the user would only get a small shock and not come to any harm.

FIG 5.10 Metal-bodied appliances should be earthed

FIG 5.11 Plastic-bodied appliances do not need to be earthed

An electrical appliance that has a plastic body does not need to be earthed because plastic is an insulator. Such appliances are described as **double insulated**.

Check your understanding

1.

FIG 5.12 Gabriella's hairdryer

a) How does Gabriella connect her hairdryer to the power supply?

b) Why should Gabriella not use her hairdryer when her hands are wet?

c) What is the outer casing made of?

d) Will Gabriella's hairdryer have a 2-pin or a 3-pin plug? Explain your answer.

Fun fact

Electricians use a detector to locate electrical wiring in walls and floors to avoid accidentally drilling through a cable and getting an electric shock.

Key terms

earth wire wire in a plug that is connected to the metal body of the appliance to protect the user in the event of a fault

double insulated an appliance that has a body made of an insulating material

Complete circuit

We are learning how to:

- construct simple electrical circuits
- identify a complete circuit.

Complete circuit »»

We use mains electricity to power most appliances in our homes but it is far too dangerous for building circuits in the laboratory. Instead we use a **cell** or a **battery**. They provide much less electrical energy than the mains supply.

You might use the words 'cell' and 'battery' to mean the same thing in everyday language but in science these terms have particular meanings. A cell is what is often incorrectly called a battery, and a battery is a combination of two or more cells.

FIG 5.13 This is a single cell

Activity 5.3

Building simple circuits

Here is what you need:

- cell in holder
- lamp
- connecting wires.

Here is what you should do:

1. Make the circuit shown in Fig 5.15.

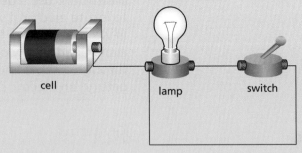

cell

lamp   switch

FIG 5.15

2. Draw the circuit and, alongside, say whether the lamp lit up or not when the switch was closed.

3. Make up five more different circuits.

4. Make a drawing of each circuit and say whether the lamp lights or not when the switch is closed.

5. Look at the circuits you made in which the lamp lit up. Can you see anything similar about them?

FIG 5.14 When two or more cells are used together to power an electrical device they are called a battery

A **circuit** is a complete pathway around which an electric current can flow. The pathway must be made of a conductor such as a metal wire.

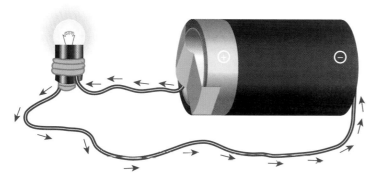

FIG 5.16 Direction of conventional current

A cell has a positive (+) terminal and a negative (–) terminal. Conventionally, the direction of the electric current is taken to flow from the positive terminal to the negative terminal. This is called **conventional current flow.**

In reality, the current is the result of a flow of electrons. Since electrons carry a negative charge, they actually flow from the negative terminal (where there are a lot of negative charges) to the positive terminal of the cell (where there are fewer negative charges). This is called **electron flow** and is in the opposite direction to the conventional current.

Check your understanding

1.

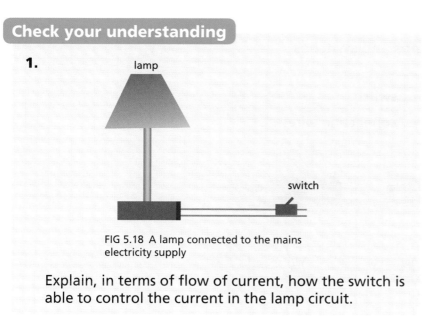

FIG 5.18 A lamp connected to the mains electricity supply

Explain, in terms of flow of current, how the switch is able to control the current in the lamp circuit.

Fun fact

You can create electricity using fruit and rods of two different metals, such as zinc and copper. Juicy fruits such as limes, oranges or lemons work best.

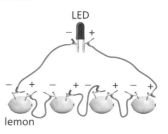

FIG 5.17 A fruit battery

Each lemon is a cell. When several are connected together, they produce enough electricity to light a small device called a light emitting diode (LED).

Key terms

cell electrical power source often incorrectly called a battery

battery a combination of two or more cells

circuit a complete pathway around which an electric current can flow

conventional current flow current taken to flow from the positive terminal to the negative terminal of a cell

electron flow electrons flow from the negative terminal to the positive terminal of a cell

Cells and lamps

We are learning how to:

- construct simple electrical circuits
- observe the effect of using different numbers of cells and lamps in a circuit.

Cells and lamps »»

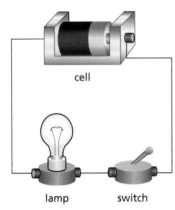

FIG 5.19 A simple lighting circuit might consist of a cell, a lamp and a switch

When additional components are added to a circuit, they can often be added in different ways, with different results.

Activity 5.4

Making circuits with cells, lamps and switches

Here is what you need:

- two cells
- two lamps
- switch
- connecting wires.

Here is what you should do:

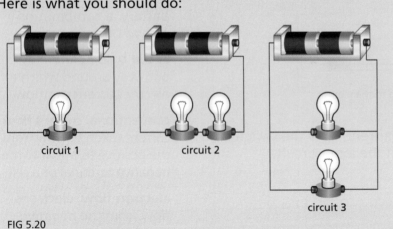

FIG 5.20

1. Build circuit 1.

2. Reverse the direction of one of the cells in circuit 1. Does the lamp still light up?

3. Build circuit 2 and make a note of how brightly the lamps glow.

4. Build circuit 3.

5. Do the lamps in circuit 3 glow less brightly, as brightly or more brightly than in circuit 2?

6. Include a switch at some different places in circuit 3. Do the lamps turn on and off differently according to the position of the switch?

There is a difference in potential energy (**potential difference**) between the terminals of a cell. This is measured in **volts (V)**. A single cell has a potential difference of 1.5 V, which is usually written on the side of it.

a)

1.5 V + 1.5 V = 3.0 V

b)

1.5 V − 1.5 V = 0.0 V

FIG 5.21 **a)** When two cells are arranged so that their positive terminals point in the same direction, the overall potential difference of the battery is the sum of the potential differences of the cells, i.e. 3.0 V

b) When cells are arranged so that their positive terminals point in opposite directions, the overall potential difference of the battery is the difference between the potential differences of the cells, i.e. 0 V

lamps in series

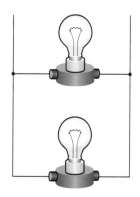

lamps in parallel

FIG 5.22 Two lamps can be connected in a circuit in two different ways

Key terms

potential difference difference in potential energy between two points

volts (V) units of potential difference

Check your understanding

1. Draw a circuit containing two cells, two lamps and one switch so that both lamps are on when the switch is closed and one lamp remains on when the switch is open.

Measuring current

We are learning how to:

- construct simple electrical circuits
- measure current using an ammeter.

Measuring current ⟩⟩

The amount of current passing in a circuit is measured using an **ammeter**. The unit of current is the **ampere (amp, symbol A)**.

In the activities we carry out in the laboratory, the current is often less than 1 ampere so we measure current in milliamperes or mA. There are 1000 milliamperes in 1 ampere.

$$1 \text{ A} = 1000 \text{ mA}$$

Electric current is measured by an ammeter. There are two types in common use.

An analogue ammeter has a moving pointer and the current is read from a scale where the pointer stops. A digital ammeter gives a direct numerical readout. It may be part of a **multimeter**, which has many different uses.

a)

b)

FIG 5.23 **a)** Analogue ammeter
b) Digital ammeter

Activity 5.5

Measuring the current at different points in a circuit

Here is what you need:

- battery containing two cells
- three lamps
- ammeter
- connecting wires
- long length of nichrome wire
- crocodile clip.

Here is what you should do:

1. Build the circuit shown in Fig 5.25.

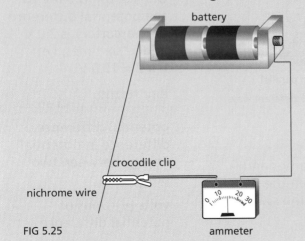

battery

crocodile clip

nichrome wire

FIG 5.25

ammeter

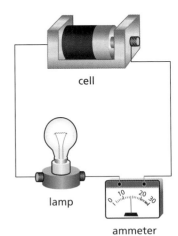

cell

lamp

ammeter

FIG 5.24 An ammeter is always connected in series to the component whose current it is measuring

2. Connect the ammeter to different points on the nichrome wire using a crocodile clip.

3. How does the reading on the ammeter change with changes in the length of the nichrome wire in the circuit?

4. Build the circuit shown in Fig 5.26.

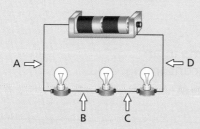

FIG 5.26

5. Connect the ammeter at point A in the circuit and record the current.

6. Repeat this at points B, C and D, recording the current each time.

7. What can you say about the current at different points in a series circuit?

Nichrome wire resists the flow of current in a circuit. The greater the length of nichrome wire included in a circuit, the smaller the current that flows through it.

When components such as lamps are connected in series in a circuit, the current is the same no matter where in the circuit it is measured.

Check your understanding

1. **a)** What is the reading on the ammeter:

   i) in milliamperes?

   ii) in amperes?

   b) Draw a diagram to show how an ammeter should be placed in a circuit containing a battery of two cells and one lamp, so that the current flowing through the lamp can be measured.

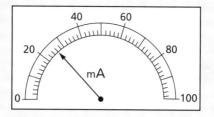

FIG 5.27 The reading on a milliammeter

Key terms

ammeter instrument used to measure current in a circuit

ampere (amp, symbol A) unit of current

multimeter instrument used to measure current and other properties of a circuit

Circuit symbols

We are learning how to:

- represent simple circuits using diagrams
- identify components of an electrical circuit from their symbols.

Circuit symbols ⟫

It would be possible to draw all of the **components** in an electrical circuit diagram but this would be time-consuming. It is much easier to draw the circuit using **symbols** to represent each of the components.

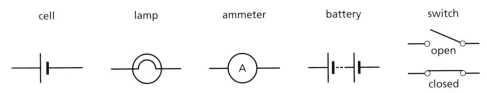

FIG 5.28 These symbols for components are used and understood by scientists all over the world

Notice that the symbol for a cell has two vertical lines. The long thin line represents the positive (+) terminal and the shorter thicker line represents the negative (–) terminal. It is important that you draw the symbol in the correct direction in a circuit diagram.

To draw a **circuit diagram** we draw the appropriate symbols and then connect them together by lines to represent connecting wires.

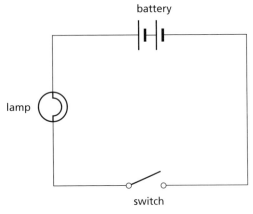

FIG 5.29 A circuit diagram for a circuit containing a battery, a lamp and a switch all connected in series

Notice that if a battery is composed of several cells, repeating the symbol for a cell can be tedious. It is much easier to join the symbols for two cells by a dashed line.

FIG 5.30 How to represent a battery composed of six cells

Activity 5.6

Drawing circuit diagrams

You will not need any equipment or materials for this activity.

Here is what you should do:

1. Look back at Fig 5.24 and redraw the circuit using suitable symbols.

2. Look back at Fig 5.25 and redraw the circuit using suitable symbols.

3. Look back at Fig 5.26 and redraw the circuit using suitable symbols.

4. Would you say that it is easier to draw circuits using symbols than drawing the components?

5. Would you say that circuits drawn in symbols are easier to understand than circuits in which the components are drawn?

Check your understanding

1. Name the components in this electrical circuit.

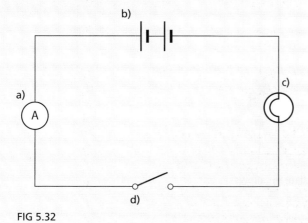

FIG 5.32

2. Draw a circuit diagram containing a battery of three cells, two lamps and a switch connected in series.

Fun fact

There are two symbols commonly used to represent a lamp in circuit diagrams.

lamp as a source of light   lamp as an indicator

FIG 5.31 Symbols for a lamp

One symbol is used when the lamp is a source of light, such as in a torch circuit. The other is used when the lamp is an indicator of some kind, such as a light that comes on when an appliance is in use.

Key terms

components parts of a circuit

symbols signs used to represent something

circuit diagram diagram showing how components in a circuit are connected

Constructing circuits from circuit diagrams

We are learning how to:

* represent simple circuits using diagrams
* construct a circuit from a circuit diagram.

Constructing circuits from circuit diagrams ⟫⟫

To build a circuit we need to examine a circuit diagram in order to:

* identify the electrical components

* determine how the components are connected together.

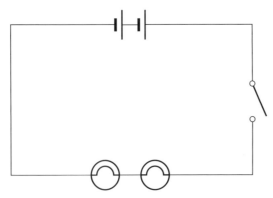

FIG 5.33 The symbols show that the circuit contains: two cells, two lamps and one switch connected in series

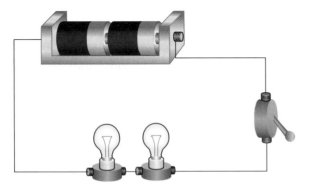

FIG 5.34 The information from the circuit diagram allows us to build the actual circuit

Building circuits from circuit diagrams

Here is what you need:

- three cells
- two lamps
- two switches
- ammeter
- connecting wires.

Here is what you should do:

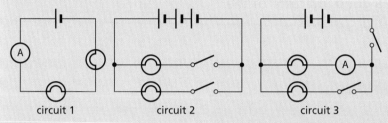

circuit 1   circuit 2   circuit 3

FIG 5.35

1. Select the components you will need to build circuit 1 and connect them together as shown in the diagram.

2. Check your circuit with the circuit diagram to make sure they are the same.

3. Repeat this for circuit 2 and then circuit 3.

Check your understanding

1. Fig 5.36 is a circuit diagram.

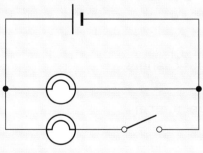

FIG 5.36

What components are needed to build this circuit (not including connecting wires)?

Fun fact

Sometimes wires may cross over each other in a circuit but may not actually join together.

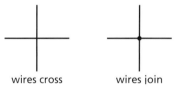

wires cross   wires join

FIG 5.37 In order to show the difference between wires that cross and wires that join in a circuit diagram, we place a dot where wires join

Connecting components in series

We are learning how to:

- represent simple circuits using diagrams
- connect components in series in a circuit.

Connecting components in series ⟩⟩

The brightness of a lamp is determined by how much electrical energy is being converted to light (and heat) energy. The brightness is therefore a good indicator of the amount of current passing.

Activity 5.8

Investigating bulbs connected in series

Here is what you need:

- battery containing three cells
- four lamps
- ammeter
- connecting wires.

Here is what you should do:

1. Connect a single lamp in series with an ammeter in a circuit.

2. Note the brightness of the lamp and the reading on the ammeter.

3. Repeat this for two, three and four lamps connected in series and, in addition, find out what happens when one lamp is partially unscrewed from its holder so it goes out.

4. Record your observations in a table.

5. Comment on how the brightness of the lamps changes as the number of lamps increases.

6. Comment on how the current changes as the number of lamps increases.

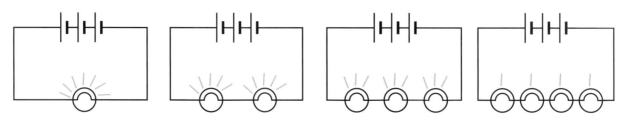

FIG 5.38 What happens when increasing numbers of lamps are connected in series?

As more lamps are added to the circuit, the lamps shine less brightly. If an ammeter is included in each circuit, it will show that the current falls as the number of lamps increases.

Lamps in **series** are connected by a single circuit. If there is a break in the circuit, such as will occur if one of the lamps burns out or is removed, then the circuit is no longer complete and all the lamps will go out.

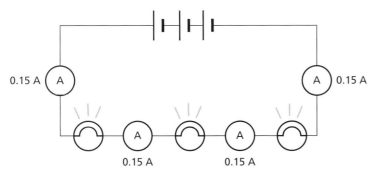

FIG 5.39 When lamps are connected in series it does not matter where the ammeter is positioned as the current through the circuit is the same at all points (in this circuit the current is 0.15 A)

Single components are often connected in series with a switch to control them. For example, a torch consists of a lamp in series with a switch to turn it on and off. Many household appliances are connected in a similar way.

Check your understanding

1. Fig 5.40 shows a circuit in which three lamps are connected in series. The reading on the ammeter is 0.12 A.

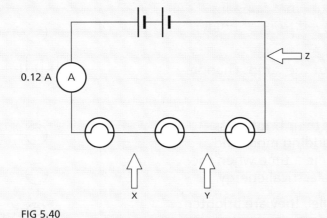

FIG 5.40

a) How would the brightness of the lamps change, if at all, if another lamp was added in series?

b) At which of the points X, Y and Z in the circuit would the current be 0.12 A?

c) What would be the reading on the ammeter if one of the lamps burned out? Explain your answer.

Fun fact

When identical cells are connected in series in a battery, the potential difference across the battery is the sum of the potential differences of the cells, provided they are connected in the same direction.

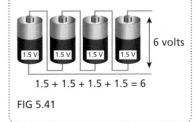

1.5 + 1.5 + 1.5 + 1.5 = 6

FIG 5.41

Key term

series way of connecting components so that they are in one loop in the circuit

101

Connecting components in parallel

We are learning how to:

- represent simple circuits using diagrams
- connect components in parallel in a circuit.

Connecting components in parallel 》》

An electric current only flows through a complete circuit. When two components are connected in **parallel** there are effectively two circuits with a part that is common to both components.

Activity 5.9

Investigating lamps connected in parallel

Here is what you need:

- battery containing three cells
- four lamps
- connecting wires.

Here is what you should do:

1. Connect a single lamp in a circuit.

2. Note the brightness of the lamp.

3. Repeat this for two, three and four lamps connected in parallel and, in addition, find out what happens when one lamp is partially unscrewed from its holder so it goes out.

4. Comment on how the brightness of the lamps changes as the number increases.

Adding lamps in parallel does not alter their brightness. However, it is not possible to keep on adding more and more lamps without end. There will come a time when the battery is unable to provide sufficient electrical energy.

When two lamps are connected in parallel, they are brighter than they would be if they were connected in series, but they draw twice as much current from the battery. This means that the battery will be exhausted more quickly. Two lamps connected in series will shine less brightly but will continue to shine for longer because the battery will last for longer.

Components are connected in parallel so they can be controlled independently. For example, a hairdryer may

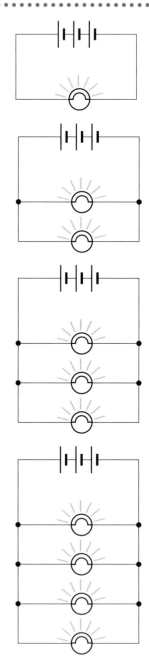

FIG 5.42 What happens when increasing numbers of lamps are connected in parallel?

have a variable heater and a variable fan. These are wired in parallel so the heat and the blow functions can be controlled separately.

Components connected in parallel don't all fail if one component ceases working. For example, Christmas lights continue to work even when some of the bulbs burn out and need replacing.

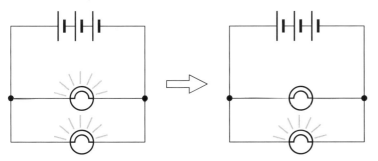

FIG 5.43 When lamps are connected in parallel, if one breaks, the circuit containing the second lamp remains complete and so the second lamp remains lit

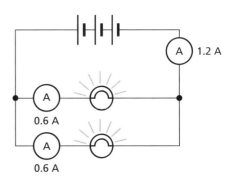

FIG 5.44 If ammeters are at different positions in the same circuit, the total current flowing from the battery is equal to the sum of the currents passing through each bulb, so here the values are 0.6 A + 0.6 A = 1.2 A

Check your understanding

1.

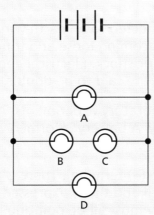

FIG 5.45 Four similar lamps connected to a battery

Copy and complete the table to show which lamps would remain on and which would go off when each of the lamps burned out.

Lamp that is burned out	Lamp goes out or remains on			
	A	B	C	D
A	off			
B		off		
C			off	
D				off

TABLE 5.1

Fun fact

When identical cells are connected in parallel, the potential difference across them is the same as the potential difference across one cell provided they are connected in the same direction.

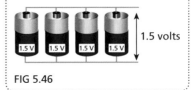

FIG 5.46

Key term

parallel way of connecting components in a circuit so that the potential difference is the same across all branches of the circuit

Review of Electricity

- Electricity is a convenient form of energy that is transferred from place to place as an electric current. A typical household uses many devices that are powered by electricity.

  - Materials that conduct an electric current are called electrical conductors. All metals are good conductors.

  - Materials that do not conduct an electric current are called electrical insulators. These include plastic, wood, glass, rubber and card.

- Metals are good conductors because they contain delocalised electrons. These particles carry electrical charge along the metal. Insulating materials do not contain delocalised electrons.

- Electricity is potentially dangerous so electrical devices must be handled with care. An electrical appliance is connected to a plug. The plug fits into a socket, which provides electricity. Electricity users should not:

  - poke objects into sockets

  - use appliances that have damaged plugs

  - handle appliances with wet hands.

- Electrical appliances with metal bodies are connected to an earth wire. This provides a pathway for the current in the event of wires coming loose and touching the metal body. This protects the user from a severe electric shock. Electrical appliances with plastic bodies do not require an earth wire and are said to be double insulated.

- Mains electricity is too dangerous for use in laboratory experiments. A cell is a means of providing a small and safe amount of energy. A battery is formed when two or more cells are joined together.

- A cell has a positive (+) terminal and a negative (–) terminal. There is a difference in potential energy between the terminals of a cell and this is expressed in volts. When cells are placed together to form a battery, they must all be pointing in the same direction, that is the positive terminal of one cell is connected to the negative terminal of another cell.

- The conventional current in a circuit flows from the positive terminal of a cell or battery through the circuit to the negative terminal. The flow of electrons, which carry electrical charge, is in the opposite direction.

- A complete circuit is needed for an electric current to flow. The current stops if there is a break in the circuit. A switch is a device that can be used to turn a device on and off by completing or breaking the circuit.

- An electric current can be measured using an ammeter. The unit of current is the ampere, A, or for smaller currents, the milliampere, mA. There are 1000 milliamperes in 1 ampere.

- A circuit diagram is a method of representing a circuit by a series of connected symbols. Each symbol represents a component in the circuit. Circuit diagrams are quick to draw and are universally understood because scientists around the world use the same symbols.

- In order to build a circuit from a circuit diagram we must:
  - identify the electrical components
  - determine how the components are connected together.

- Components in a circuit can be connected in series or in parallel.

- When lamps are connected in series the more lamps there are, the dimmer they are and the less current flows in the circuit.

- When lamps are connected in parallel they shine with the brightness of a single lamp up to the point where the cell or battery cannot provide any more electrical energy. The current passing through the whole circuit is equal to the sum of the current passing through each lamp.

- Lamps connected in parallel are brighter than lamps connected in series but they draw more current from the battery. This means that the battery will be exhausted more quickly. Lamps connected in series will shine less brightly but will continue to shine for longer because the battery will last for longer.

Review questions on Electricity

1. Redraw the circuit in Fig 5.47 as a circuit diagram, using appropriate symbols for the components.

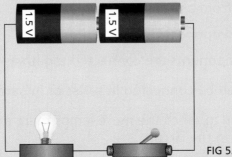

FIG 5.47

2. Dante used the circuit shown in Fig 5.48 to test whether materials conduct electricity.

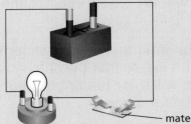

material   FIG 5.48

a) How was Dante able to decide whether or not each material conducted electricity?

b) Before testing the materials, Dante connected the two crocodile clips together. Why did he do this?

c) Here is a list of the materials Dante tested. Arrange them in groups according to whether or not they conduct electricity.

copper   cardboard   plastic   iron
wood   glass   steel   lead

d) What name is given to a material that does not conduct electricity?

e) Give one common feature of all of the materials that conduct electricity.

3. Fig 5.49 shows the inside of the electric plug fitted to an electric iron.

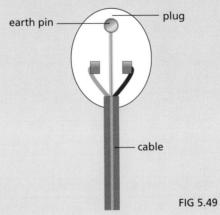

earth pin — plug

cable

FIG 5.49

a) **i)** How many wires are in the cable?

    ii) Which colour wire goes to the earth pin?

b) The cable of a plastic-bodied reading lamp only has two wires.

    i) Which wire is missing?

    ii) Why is it not needed?

c) Part of the plastic top of the plug has broken off.

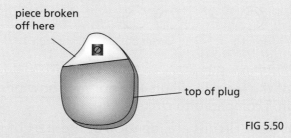

FIG 5.50

Is the plug still safe to use? Explain your answer.

4. Fig 5.51 shows a circuit containing a cell, two lamps and an ammeter.

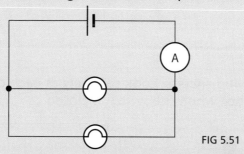

FIG 5.51

State whether each of the following circuits is equivalent to the above circuit or not.

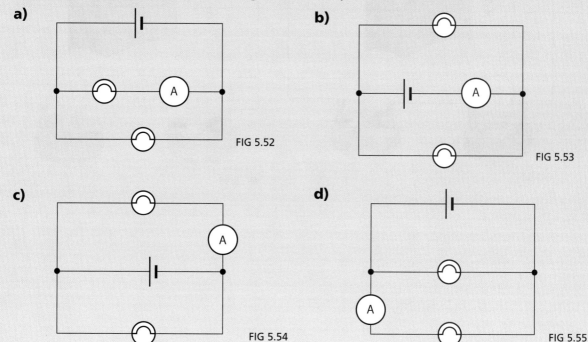

a)

FIG 5.52

b)

FIG 5.53

c)

FIG 5.54

d)

FIG 5.55

5. Fig 5.56 shows an experiment using some circuits containing identical lamps.

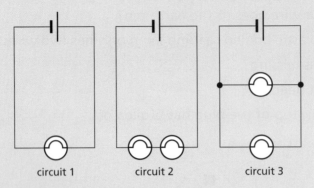

circuit 1   circuit 2   circuit 3

FIG 5.56

a) If the brightness of the lamp in circuit 1 is 'normal', how bright are the lamps in circuit 2 and circuit 3 compared to circuit 1?

b) If the cells used in these circuits are identical at the start of the experiment, how long will the cell in circuit 2 and in circuit 3 last compared to the cell in circuit 1?

c) Explain what will happen if one of the lamps burns out in:

   i) circuit 2

   ii) circuit 3.

6. Shivana made the following circuits. Look carefully at each one and say whether the bulb would come on or not when the switch is closed.

a)   b)

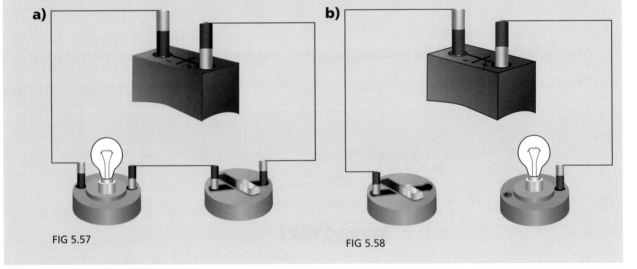

FIG 5.57   FIG 5.58

c)

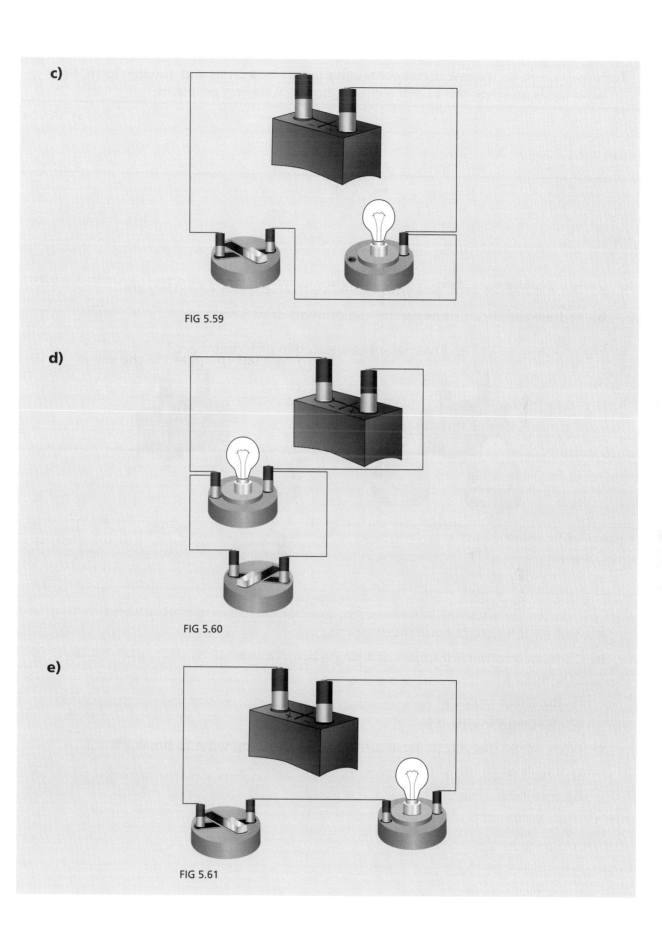

FIG 5.59

d)

FIG 5.60

e)

FIG 5.61

109

7. Fareed wants to make a circuit containing two cells, a lamp and a switch so that the lamp lights up when the switch is closed, but he is having problems.

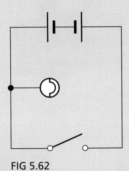

FIG 5.62

a) There are three problems with Fareed's circuit. Explain what they are.

b) Redraw the circuit showing the components drawn correctly.

8. Fig 5.63 shows a cell and two lamps connected in different ways.

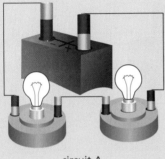

circuit A

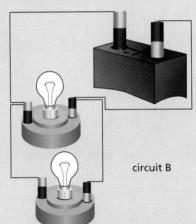

circuit B

FIG 5.63

a) Redraw the circuits as circuit diagrams.

b) Compared to the brightness of a single lamp connected to a cell, describe the brightness of:

  i) the lamps in circuit A

  ii) the lamps in circuit B.

c) What would happen to the second lamp if one lamp were to break in:

  i) circuit A?

  ii) circuit B?

9. Fig 5.64 shows the components inside a toy car.

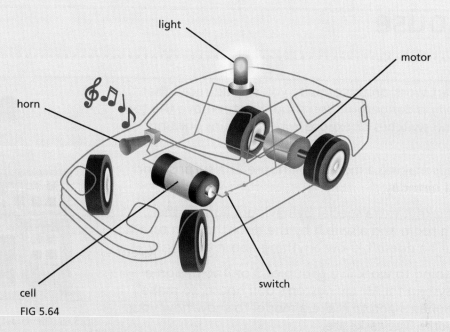

light

motor

horn

switch

cell

FIG 5.64

a) Which of the labelled components provides the car with energy?

b) Draw a circuit diagram showing how the components are connected together. Make up suitable symbols for the horn and the motor.

c) If the horn in the toy car broke, would the lamp still work? Explain your answer.

Lighting up a model doll house

Before you start work on this activity you should recall that mains electricity is dangerous. You should not remove the tops from lamps and switches or expose wires in mains lighting circuits.

Mr Livingston is making a model doll house as a surprise for his daughter's birthday.

He wants to make it extra special by having a light in the ceiling of each room and a switch by the door that can turn it on and off but he doesn't know anything about electricity.

FIG 5.65 The model doll house Mr Livingston is making

1. You are going to work in a group of 3 or 4 to design a lighting system for Mr Livingston's doll house, to make the components and to make a model to show how your system works. The tasks are:

   - to research about house lighting
   - to design a suitable lighting circuit
   - to design and make 'lamps' and 'switches' to a suitable scale for a doll house
   - to build a model of a doll house out of cardboard
   - to install your lighting system in your model
   - to test your lighting system
   - to consider how your lighting system might be modified or extended.

a) Take a look at how the lighting is arranged in your home.

   In each room the switch only controls the light for that room.

   Use your knowledge of series and parallel circuits to design a suitable lighting circuit for a doll house that contains four rooms.

b) Even small torch bulbs are too big for a doll house. You need to find lights which are even smaller than these.

   One possibility is light-emitting diodes. These are not bulbs but components that shine when a current passes through them. You have probably seen red LEDs on electrical equipment. They are often used to show something is switched on. They come in three different sizes: 3 mm, 5 mm and 10 mm, so you will need to choose which is appropriate for the scale of your model.

FIG 5.66 Room light and switch

If you use LEDs there are two important things you must take into account:

- LEDs cannot be connected directly to cells or they will burn out instantly. They must be wired in series with a resistor. You will need to carry out research to determine the size of the resistor.
- LEDs must be connected in a circuit so that the longer pin is connected to the positive side of the cell or battery otherwise they will not work.

Similarly, household switches are far too large for a doll house so you will have to design and make your own.

The examples of 'homemade' switches might give you some ideas. You will need to make a switch for each room of the model doll house.

c) Build a model of a doll house using a cardboard box and cardboard dividers for the walls.

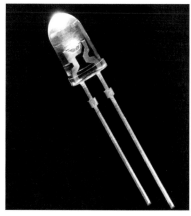

FIG 5.67 Light-emitting diode or LED

Your model doesn't have to be very detailed as you are only going to use it to demonstrate your lighting system.

d) Install your lighting system into your model and test it to make sure the light in each room turns on and off without affecting the lights in the other rooms. Use a battery to power your lights.

e) Consider how you might modify or extend your lighting system. For example:

- you might install two switches in one room so that the light could be controlled from either switch; this is the sort of arrangement that you see in hallways and staircases
- you might install two lights in one room controlled by only one switch.

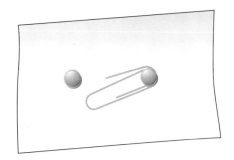

FIG 5.68 'Homemade' switches

f) Prepare a PowerPoint presentation in which you will describe your lighting circuit, explain how you made lights and switches, and demonstrate the lighting circuit installed on your model. You should also be ready to discuss how your lighting circuit could be modified to provide different arrangements of lights and switches.

FIG 5.69 Model doll house

Unit 6: Magnetism

Magnetism >>

People have known about magnetism for thousands of years. Lodestone is a naturally occurring mineral that is magnetic. This mineral attracts objects made of iron.

FIG 6.1 If a piece of lodestone is suspended by a thread and spun, when it stops it is always pointing in the same direction

The name 'lodestone' means leading stone. It is an early form of a compass.

Magnetic and non-magnetic materials

Some materials, such as iron, are described as magnetic because they are attracted to a magnet. Other materials, such as copper and plastic, are non-magnetic.

FIG 6.2 Magnetism is used to separate metals in a scrapyard. Metals such as iron and steel become attached to a magnet while other metals such as copper and aluminium are left behind

Magnets

Magnets come in all shapes and sizes.

FIG 6.3 **a)** Bar magnet **b)** Horseshoe magnet

All magnets have two poles, which are traditionally called the north pole, N, and the south pole, S. The two poles of a magnet look the same so, to help identify them, magnets are sometimes painted red for the N pole and blue for the S pole.

Magnets have invisible magnetic field lines surrounding them. The poles of two magnets interact in an unusual way, which we call the law of magnetic poles.

Electromagnets

When a current is passed along a conductor, such as a wire, a magnetic field is generated.

Magnets created by passing an electric current are called electromagnets. They have magnetic poles and magnetic field lines just like other magnets.

Something to think about

Fig 6.4 is a picture of an early Chinese device used by travellers.

FIG 6.4 The object that looks like a spoon is made of lodestone and is able to turn on the metal disc underneath

Magnetic and non-magnetic materials

We are learning how to:

- demonstrate the effects of magnetic forces
- determine whether a material is magnetic or not.

Magnetic and non-magnetic materials ⟩⟩

Lodestone is an oxide of iron and is also called magnetite.

Materials such as iron and steel, that are attracted to a magnet, are described as **magnetic**, while materials such as brass, copper and aluminium, that are not attracted to a magnet, are described as **non-magnetic**.

FIG 6.5 Lodestone, a type of rock, attracts objects made of iron, such as nails and bolts

Activity 6.1

Magnetic and non-magnetic materials

Here is what you need:

- magnet
- objects made of different materials, e.g. nail, paper clip, plastic ruler, eraser.

Here is what you should do:

1. Place one end of the magnet near an object and find out if the material is attracted to it.

2. Materials that are attracted by a magnet are described as magnetic materials.

3. Test each object in turn with the magnet.

4. Display your observations in a table. On one side of the table list the magnetic materials and on the other side list the non-magnetic materials.

Permanent magnets

Materials that keep their magnetism for a long time are called permanent magnets.

Materials that have permanent magnetism are iron, mild steel, cobalt and nickel. Modern magnets are often made of special alloys containing these metals such as alnico and alcomax.

Ceramic or ferrite magnets are made by baking iron oxide and other metal oxides in a ceramic matrix.

FIG 6.7 The element neodymium forms alloys with iron and boron that are used to make powerful permanent magnets

FIG 6.6 Ceramic magnets can be made in any shape but have the disadvantage that they are brittle, so if they are dropped on a hard surface they will break into pieces

Fun fact

An alloy is a mixture of a metallic element with one or more other elements that may be metals or non-metals. Steel is an alloy of iron and carbon.

Sometimes alloys have more useful properties than the elements from which they are formed. For example, alnico is an alloy of aluminium, nickel and cobalt. It makes more powerful magnets than the pure metals.

Key terms

magnetic materials such as iron and steel that are attracted to a magnet

non-magnetic materials such as brass, copper and aluminium that are not attracted to a magnet

Check your understanding

1. Arrange the following metals into two groups: those that are magnetic and those that are not magnetic.

| cobalt | copper | gold | iron |
| magnesium | nickel | steel | zinc |

Law of magnetic poles

We are learning how to:

- demonstrate the effects of magnetic forces
- predict whether two magnetic poles will attract or repel each other.

Law of magnetic poles ≫

A magnet has two **poles**: a north pole and a south pole. The north and south poles are usually represented by the letters 'N' and 'S'.

Forces exist between magnets and are concentrated at the poles. The interaction between two magnets depends on the nature of the poles that are brought together.

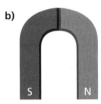

bar magnet   horseshoe magnet

FIG 6.8 **a)** Bar magnets are commonly used in the laboratory
b) A horseshoe magnet is simply a bar magnet that has been bent into the shape of a horseshoe

Activity 6.2

Law of magnetic poles

Here is what you need:

- two cotton loops
- two bar magnets
- pencil
- heavy book.

Here is what you should do:

1. Place a heavy book on top of a pencil so that the pencil is sticking out from the table.

2. Suspend a bar magnet from the pencil using loops of cotton so that it can turn freely.

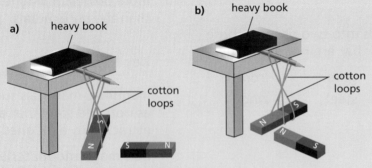

FIG 6.9 **a)** Unlike poles **b)** Like poles

3. Bring the N pole of the second magnet towards the N pole of the suspended magnet and record what happens.

4. Bring the N pole of the second magnet towards the S pole of the suspended magnet and record what happens.

5. Repeat steps 3 and 4 but using the S pole of the second magnet.

6. What deductions are you able to make about magnets from your observations?

If one magnet is suspended so it is free to rotate and a second magnet is brought near it:

- if they are **unlike poles**, that is N and S or S and N, the magnets will attract (move towards each other)

- if they are **like poles**, that is N and N or S and S, the magnets will repel (move away from each other).

Check your understanding

1. A compass needle is a magnet. The north pole of the compass always points towards the Earth's magnetic north pole, and the south pole of the compass points towards the Earth's magnetic south pole.

What is the polarity of each of the Earth's magnetic poles? Explain your answer.

FIG 6.10 Compass

Fun fact

It is impossible to say if an iron bar is magnetic or not on the basis of whether it is attracted by a magnet.

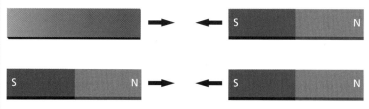

FIG 6.11 A magnet would attract an iron bar even if the iron bar were not itself a magnet

FIG 6.12 Repulsion proves an iron bar is a magnet

To test whether an iron bar is a magnet, both ends must be placed near the same magnetic pole of a magnet. If one end is repelled, this proves that the bar is a magnet.

Key terms

pole the end of the magnet

unlike poles two poles that are different, for example, north and south

like poles two poles that are the same, for example, north and north

Magnetic fields

We are learning how to:

- demonstrate the effects of magnetic forces
- draw the magnetic field around a bar magnet.

Magnetic fields >>>

A magnet is surrounded by a pattern of invisible **magnetic field lines**. We can investigate the nature of the field lines using a small plotting compass.

Activity 6.3

Magnetic field around a bar magnet

Here is what you need:

- bar magnet
- plotting compass
- plain paper.

Here is what you should do:

1. Place a bar magnet at the centre of a piece of plain paper and draw around it.
2. Remove the magnet and mark the N and S poles on the outline.
3. Place the magnet back on the outline.
4. Place the plotting compass near the north pole of the magnet. Mark two dots on the paper corresponding to the ends of the plotting compass needle.
5. Move the compass a little bit away towards the south pole and repeat drawing the dots.
6. Repeat this procedure until a circle is formed around the magnet.

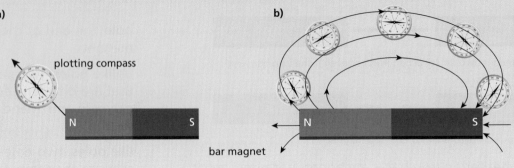

FIG 6.13

7. Connect all the dots with a smooth curve. This curve is one magnetic field line. Try to obtain four curves on each side of the magnet.

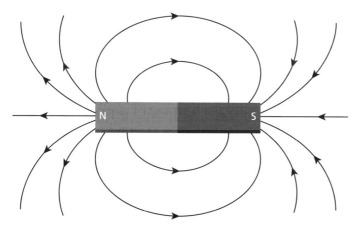

FIG 6.14 The magnetic field around a magnet can be represented by a set of magnetic field lines

Magnetic field lines are conventionally shown moving away from a north pole and towards a south pole and arrows are placed on the lines to show the direction of the field. When drawing or interpreting the magnetic field around a magnet you should remember that:

- magnetic field lines never cross over each other

- the **magnetic field strength** is shown by the concentration of field lines and is strongest where the field lines are most dense (at the poles)

- the magnetic force of a magnet decreases with distance from the poles.

FIG 6.16 The magnetic field lines around this bar magnet are also shown by the iron filings around the magnet

Check your understanding

1. Use what you have learned about the magnetic field lines around a bar magnet to draw the magnetic field between the two poles of a horseshoe magnet.

Fun fact

When two like poles are brought together, the field lines from each magnet run away from each other. At the centre of the combined magnetic fields is a null point at which there is no net magnetic field.

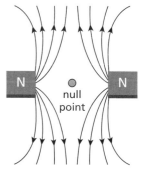

FIG 6.15 Magnetic field lines for unlike poles

The pattern of magnetic field lines for two S poles is the same as Fig 6.15, but the field lines run in the opposite direction.

Key terms

magnetic field lines a pattern of invisible lines that shows how the strength and direction of the magnetic field varies around a magnet

magnetic field strength how strong the magnetic field is at a particular point

Magnetic effect of an electric current

We are learning how to:

- describe the magnetic effect of current
- make an electromagnet.

Magnetic effect of an electric current ⟫

When a compass needle is placed close to a wire, and then a current is passed through the wire, the compass needle is deflected.

This is called the **magnetic effect of a current**.

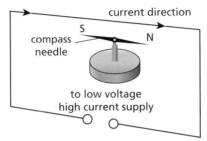

FIG 6.17 The magnetic effect of an electric current

Activity 6.4

Magnetic field around a wire carrying a current

Here is what you need:

- thick resistance wire
- plotting compass
- plain card
- DC power source.

Here is what you should do:

1. Make a small hole in the middle of a piece of card and push the wire through it.

2. Connect the wire to a DC power source. This has a positive (+) terminal and a negative (−) terminal.

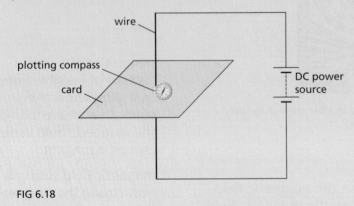

FIG 6.18

3. Place a plotting compass near the wire and show the direction that the compass points in by drawing an arrow.

4. Repeat this, placing the plotting compass in different positions until you have built up a map of the field lines around the wire.

5. Reverse the direction of the current through the wire by connecting the wire to the opposite terminals of the power source.

6. Observe if this affects the shape of the magnetic field lines around the wire and the direction of the magnetic field.

Passing a current through a conductor such as a wire creates a magnetic field consisting of a series of concentric circles. The circles are closer together nearer the wire where the magnetic field is strongest.

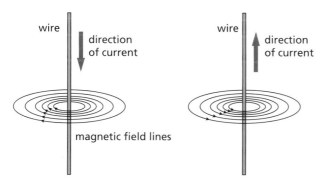

FIG 6.19 Magnetic field around a wire carrying an electric current

Reversing the direction of the current in the wire does not alter the shape of the magnetic field, but it does alter the direction of the field lines.

Check your understanding

1. Draw a diagram showing the magnetic field around a wire carrying a current viewed as if you were looking along the wire.

Fun fact

A solenoid is a coil consisting of a number of loops of wire.

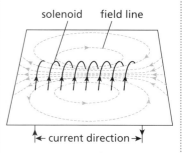

FIG 6.20 Magnetic field lines around a solenoid

The magnetic field around the solenoid is similar in shape to the magnetic field around a bar magnet.

Key term

magnetic effect of a current a compass needle is deflected when it is placed close to a wire carrying an electric current

Making an electromagnet

We are learning how to:

- describe the magnetic effect of current
- make an electromagnet.

Making an electromagnet

To make an **electromagnet** of any useful strength, you need to combine the magnetic field around many turns of wire by making a coil or solenoid.

The coils of wire on their own are magnetic when a current passes through them. However, if they are wrapped around a steel nail they make an even stronger magnet.

Activity 6.5

Making an electromagnet

Here is what you need:

- steel nail
- plastic-coated wire
- DC power source
- paper clips
- plotting compass.

Here is what you should do:

1. Take a length of wire that is coated in plastic insulation and coil it around a steel nail.

2. Make between 15 and 20 coils of wire around the nail, depending on the length of the wire.

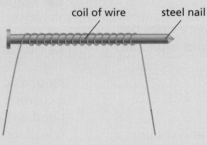

coil of wire   steel nail

FIG 6.21

3. Connect your coil to a DC power source.

4. Check that you have made an electromagnet by seeing if metal paper clips are attracted to it.

5. Place a plotting compass at different points around your electromagnet and use the direction the compass points to each time to draw a diagram of the magnetic field lines around your electromagnet.

Electromagnetism is sometimes described as temporary magnetism. An electromagnet is only magnetic while a current flows through it. If the current is turned off, the electromagnet ceases to be magnetic.

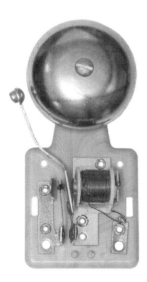

FIG 6.22 A practical electromagnet

Electromagnets used in devices such as electric bells consist of many coils of thin copper wire. At first glance the wire might not appear to be insulated, but it is. The wire is covered in a layer of lacquer, which is far less bulky than a plastic coating.

Check your understanding

1. Explain why a coil of wire can only attract paper clips when an electric current is passing through it.

Fun fact

William Sturgeon made the first electromagnet in 1824.

FIG 6.23 William Sturgeon's first electromagnet consisted of about 18 turns of varnished wire wrapped around a piece of iron in the shape of a horseshoe

Key term

electromagnet a magnet produced when a current is passed through a wire or coil of wire

Strength of an electromagnet

We are learning how to:

- describe the magnetic effect of current
- compare the strengths of different electromagnets.

Strength of an electromagnet　》》

An electromagnet is a coil of wire through which an electric current is passed. What determines the strength of an electromagnet?

- Would wrapping the coil around a piece of wooden dowel be just as good as wrapping it around a steel nail?

- Does it matter how many turns of wire are in the coil?

- Does it matter how much current you pass through the coil?

Activity 6.6

Investigating the strength of electromagnets

Here is what you need:

- steel nail
- wooden dowel
- plastic-coated wire
- DC power source
- paper clips.

Here is what you should do:

1. Take a length of wire that is coated in plastic insulation and coil it around a steel nail.

2. Make 20 coils of wire around the nail.

3. Connect your electromagnet to a DC power supply and count how many paper clips it will lift off the desk.

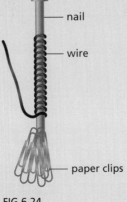

nail

wire

paper clips

FIG 6.24

4. Repeat steps 1 to 3 but use a wooden dowel in place of a steel nail.

5. Now make 10 coils of wire around a steel nail.

6. Connect your electromagnet to a DC power supply and count how many paper clips it will lift off the desk.

7. Repeat steps 2 to 6, but this time only use half of the current used previously.

8. From your observations, deduce what factors determine the strength of an electromagnet.

The strength of an electromagnet is increased by:

- wrapping the coils of wire around a core of a magnetic metal such as iron or steel

- increasing the number of turns of wire in the coil

- increasing the amount of current passing through the coil.

Check your understanding

1. Say whether each of the following statements is true or false.

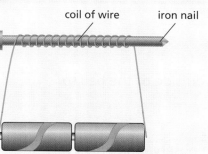

coil of wire   iron nail

FIG 6.25 An electromagnet made by wrapping wire around an iron nail and connecting it to a battery

   a) Reversing the battery will reduce the strength of the electromagnet.

   b) The iron nail would still be a strong magnet even if the battery was removed.

   c) Decreasing the number of turns of wire on the coil would reduce the strength of the electromagnet.

   d) The electromagnet would be stronger if the iron nail was removed.

   e) Wrapping the wire around two iron nails would make the electromagnet twice as strong.

   f) Connecting the coil to a battery with a higher voltage would make the electromagnet stronger.

Fun fact

Credit and debit cards have a magnetic strip containing information about the cardholder's account.

FIG 6.26 If a card with a magnetic strip is placed too near to another magnet, the magnetic field will corrupt the information and the card will no longer be of any use

Uses of permanent magnets and electromagnets

We are learning how to:

- describe the magnetic effect of current
- explain the uses of permanent magnets and electromagnets.

Uses of permanent magnets and electromagnets »»

Permanent magnets and electromagnets have many applications.

Electric bell

Activity 6.7

Investigating how an electric bell works

Here is what you need:

- electric bell
- power source
- screwdriver.

Here is what you should do:

1. Remove the cover from the outside of the bell so you can examine the parts.

2. Identify the electromagnet.

3. Turn the bell on and off and observe the effect this has on the components.

4. Use your knowledge of electric circuits and magnets to explain how the bell works.

When the bell switch is pushed the circuit is complete and the following happens:

- The electromagnet becomes magnetic.
- The electromagnet attracts the soft iron armature and the hammer strikes the gong.
- As the soft iron armature moves, the circuit is broken and the electromagnet loses its magnetism.
- The springy metal strip moves the armature back to its starting position and the cycle repeats for as long as the switch is pushed.

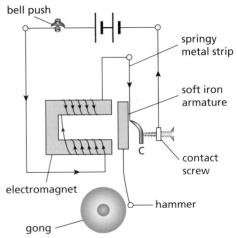

FIG 6.27 The structure of an electric doorbell

Relay

A **relay** is a switch that is operated by an electromagnet.

When a current passes between A and B, the soft iron core becomes an electromagnet. The iron armature is attracted to the electromagnet and turns on the pivot. The springy metal contacts at C are closed, completing the circuit connected across D and E.

A relay allows a circuit carrying a large current to be controlled by a second circuit carrying a small current. For example, a large current is needed to start a car engine. It is activated by the ignition switch in the car, which only carries a small current. This means that only thin wires are needed for the ignition circuit.

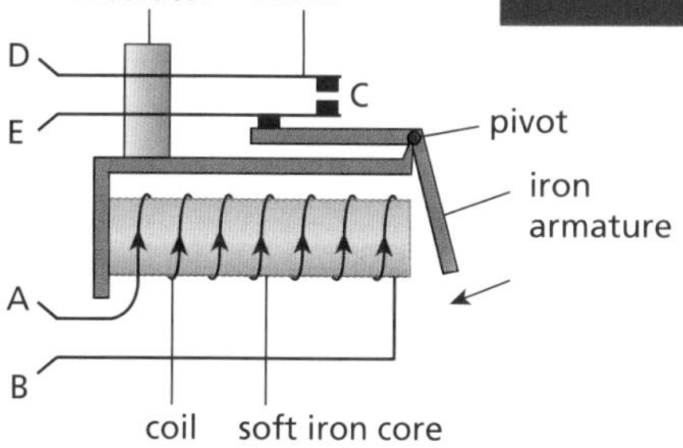

FIG 6.28 A relay allows one circuit to be controlled by another

Circuit breaker

A **circuit breaker** is a device that prevents the flow of current in a circuit in the event of a malfunction or fault.

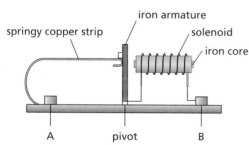

FIG 6.29 A simple circuit breaker connected to a circuit at points A and B

In the event of a fault in the circuit, the current passing through the solenoid increases. This increases the strength of the magnetic field around the **solenoid** enough for it to pull the iron **armature** towards it. When the iron armature moves towards the solenoid, the springy copper strip is released and the circuit is broken.

Fun fact

Circuit breakers are frequently used in place of fuses to protect domestic mains electricity circuits. They work much faster than fuses and can be reset simply by pushing a switch once the fault has been found and rectified.

Check your understanding

1. Explain how an electromagnet is used in an electric bell.

FIG 6.30

Key terms

relay a switch that is operated by an electromagnet

circuit breaker a device that prevents the flow of current in a circuit in the event of a fault

solenoid a cylindrical wire coil with a soft iron core inside

armature a metal part that can move to open or close a circuit

Review of Magnetism

- Lodestone or magnetite is a mineral composed of iron oxide that attracts objects made of iron. It is a naturally-occurring magnet.

- Materials that are attracted to a magnet, such as iron and steel, are described as magnetic.

- Materials such as brass, copper and aluminium, that are not attracted to a magnet, are non-magnetic.

- Materials that keep their magnetism for a long time are called permanent magnets. Examples of materials that have permanent magnetism are iron, mild steel, cobalt, nickel and special alloys containing these metals, such as alnico and alcomax.

- The law of magnetic poles states that:
  - like poles repel each other, that is N and N or S and S
  - unlike poles attract each other, that is N and S or S and N.

- It is impossible to say if an iron bar is magnetic or not on the basis of whether it is attracted by another magnet. If it is magnetic, one end should be repelled by one end of another magnet.

- A magnet is surrounded by a pattern of invisible magnetic field lines.
  - Magnetic field lines are conventionally shown to move away from a north pole and towards a south pole.
  - Magnetic field lines never cross over each other.
  - The strength of the magnetic field is shown by the concentration of field lines and is strongest where the field lines are most dense (at the poles).
  - The magnetic force of a magnet decreases with distance from the poles.

- When a current passes through a wire, a magnetic field is generated around the wire. This can be shown by placing a plotting compass near the wire. When a current is passed through the wire, the compass needle is deflected.

- The magnetic field around a wire carrying a current consists of a series of concentric circles that gradually increase in distance between each other as you move away from the wire.

- Reversing the direction of the current through a wire does not alter the shape of the magnetic field around it but it does reverse the direction of the magnetic field lines.

- An electromagnet consists of many turns of wire making a coil or solenoid.

- Electromagnetism is sometimes described as temporary magnetism because an electromagnet is only magnetic while a current flows through it. If the current is turned off, the electromagnet ceases to be magnetic.

- The strengths of different magnets can be compared by finding out how many small magnetic items, such as nails, each can lift.

- The strength of an electromagnet is increased by:
  - wrapping the coils of wire around a core of a magnetic metal such as iron or steel
  - increasing the number of turns of wire in the coil
  - increasing the amount of current passing through the coil.
- An electric bell, a relay and a circuit breaker are all common devices that contain an electromagnet.
- An electromagnet can be used to separate iron and steel from other metals in a scrapyard or recycling plant.

Review questions on Magnetism

1.

FIG 6.31 A bar magnet

Copy Fig 6.31 and draw the magnetic field lines around it. Show the direction of these field lines.

2. A bar magnet was broken into two pieces.

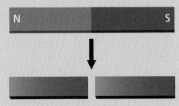

FIG 6.32

a) Copy the lower part of the diagram and show the polarity of the new ends formed.

b) Without using any other apparatus or materials, explain how you could show that both parts of the broken bar magnet have themselves become magnets.

3. Johanna was given four magnets. Her task was to compare how strong they were by counting how many small nails each could lift. Her results are shown in the table.

Magnet	Number of nails
bar magnet	3
C-shaped magnet	6
electromagnet	4
horseshoe magnet	7

TABLE 6.1

a) Which magnet was the strongest?

b) i) Which magnet could be described as a temporary magnet?

ii) Explain why.

4. Say whether each of the following will make the electromagnet stronger, weaker or have no effect.

a) Increasing the number of turns of wire

b) Decreasing the current passing through the wire

c) Putting the nail into the coil from the opposite direction

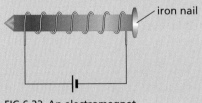

iron nail

FIG 6.33 An electromagnet

5. An investigation was carried out in which bars of three different metals, aluminium, copper and magnetised iron, were hung by a nylon thread so they could rotate freely.

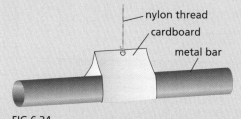

FIG 6.34

The bar was spun and then allowed to rest. Its position was then recorded. This was repeated ten times for each bar. The results are shown in Fig 6.34.

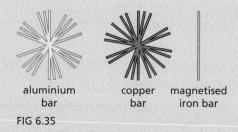

aluminium
bar

copper
bar

magnetised
iron bar

FIG 6.35

a) Describe the pattern shown by the results.

b) Explain the results.

6. Here are some statements about magnetic field lines. State whether each statement is true or false.

a) The closer together they are, the stronger the magnetic field.

b) They sometimes cross over each other.

c) They come away from a north pole and towards a south pole.

d) They are always straight lines.

e) They are not produced by electromagnets.

7. A student is given three iron bars. The ends of the bars are marked A to F.

FIG 6.36

Two of the bars are known to be magnets and the third one is not. Explain how the student can identify which bar is not a magnet using only the three bars.

8. Fig 6.38 shows an electromagnet in a circuit with three bulbs: X, Y and Z.

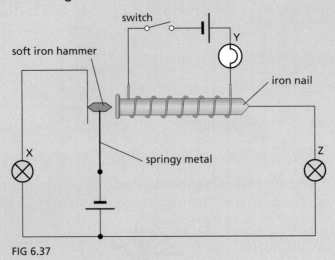

FIG 6.37

a) Copy and complete the table by indicating whether each bulb is 'off' or 'on' when the switch is open and when it is closed.

Switch	Bulb X	Bulb Y	Bulb Z
open			
closed			

b) The iron nail in the circuit is replaced by a length of wooden dowel of the same diameter.

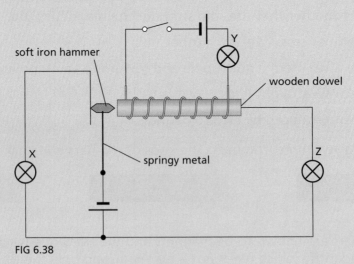

FIG 6.38

State whether each of the three bulbs will be on or off when the switch is closed. Explain your answer.

9. In a scrapyard, an electromagnet is used to separate metals.

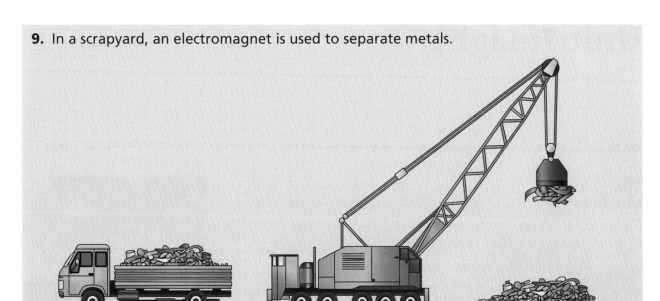

FIG 6.39

Name one metal being loaded on the truck and one that will remain on the ground.

Unit 7: Light

Light >>>

Light rays

Light is a form of energy. It travels from place to place very quickly as a beam made up of many light rays.

At night, people light up their homes using candles, paraffin lamps and electric lightbulbs.

FIG 7.1 During the day the world is lit up by light from the Sun

FIG 7.2 In towns and cities, streets and shop fronts may also be lit at night

Transparent, translucent and opaque

Materials behave differently when light shines on them. This is sometimes important in building design.

FIG 7.3 Windows are transparent because they allow light to pass through them; walls do not allow light to pass through them and they are therefore opaque

Materials such as fabrics, that let some light through, are described as translucent.

Shadows and eclipses

When an opaque object is illuminated on one side by a light source, a shadow forms on the opposite side. The shadow is an area that receives no light. The light cannot bend around the object because it only travels in straight lines.

FIG 7.4 Huge shadows, called eclipses, are cast when the Moon passes between the Sun and the Earth, or when the Earth passes between the Sun and the Moon

Reflection

We can see objects because they reflect light rays into our eyes. Reflection causes a ray of light to change direction.

Refraction

Light always travels very quickly but it travels at slightly different speeds in different materials. When a ray of light travels from one material into another, the change of speed causes a change of direction. This behaviour is called refraction.

When we look at objects in water, they appear nearer the surface than they actually are. The difference between their real depth and their apparent depth is the result of refraction.

Dispersion

Light from the Sun is actually composed of rays of many different colours that combine together to form 'white light'. When white light passes through a glass prism, the different colours are refracted by different amounts, forming a spectrum. This behaviour is called dispersion.

A rainbow is caused by the dispersion of sunlight by millions of tiny water droplets in the atmosphere. Rainbows often occur when it is raining.

Something to think about

Light rays travel at a speed of 300 000 km per second through the vacuum of space.

Although this is very fast, the Sun is so far away from the Earth that if the Sun suddenly stopped shining it would be eight and a half minutes before it all went dark on Earth.

Light rays

We are learning how to:

- investigate the transmission of light in different media
- describe simple properties of light rays.

Light rays >>>

A collection of light **rays** is called a **beam**. The light rays in a beam might or might not all be travelling in the same direction.

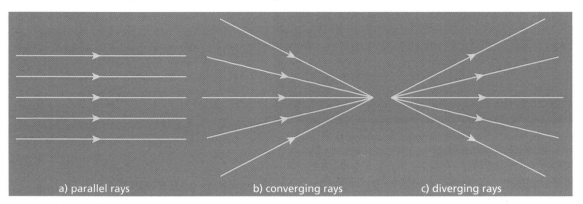

a) parallel rays   b) converging rays   c) diverging rays

FIG 7.5 A beam of **a)** parallel rays **b)** converging rays **c)** diverging rays

A beam might contain light rays that are **parallel**, that **converge** to a point or that **diverge** from a point.

Activity 7.1

Investigating whether light waves can bend around objects

Here is what you need:

- three pieces of card with a hole in the middle
- torch or candle
- modelling clay.

Here is what you should do:

1. Place the cards on the table in a line and support them with modelling clay.
2. Place the torch at one side and look through the hole in the card on the other side.
3. Move the cards until the three holes are lined up. Can you see the light from the torch?
4. Move the middle card a short way to the side. Can you still see the light from the torch?
5. What can you deduce about the way in which light waves move?

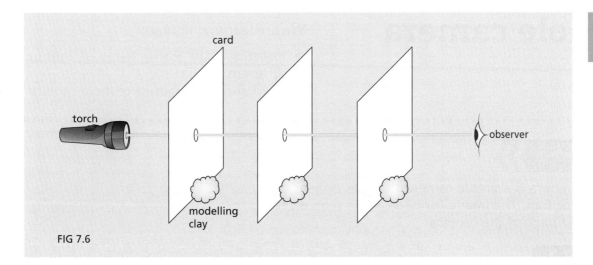

FIG 7.6

Light travels in straight lines. This is sometimes described as **rectilinear propagation**. Light waves cannot normally bend around an object.

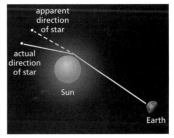
Check your understanding

1. Fig 7.7 shows the positions of four girls around a hut, as seen from above.

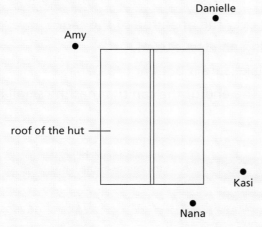

FIG 7.7

a) Copy and complete the table to show which of the other girls each girl can see.

	Amy	Danielle	Kasi	Nana
Amy				
Danielle				
Kasi				
Nana				

b) Explain how you can predict this.

Key terms

rays straight lines of light

beam a collection of light rays

parallel rays that are the same distance apart all the time

converge rays that meet at a point

diverge rays that move out from a point

rectilinear propagation travelling in straight lines

Pinhole camera

We are learning how to:

- investigate the transmission of light in different media
- build and investigate a pinhole camera.

Pinhole camera >>>

A pinhole camera is a simple camera that has no lens or photographic film. The **image** formed can be seen on the screen at the back of the camera.

Activity 7.2

Making a pinhole camera

Here is what you need:

- can or small cardboard box painted matt black inside with a small hole at the base
- greaseproof paper or parchment
- elastic band
- small candle.

 SAFETY
Take care with a lit candle.

Here is what you should do:

1. Carefully stretch the greaseproof paper over the open top of the can.
2. Hold the greaseproof paper in place using an elastic band.
3. Place the can sideways on your table. Make sure it does not roll off.
4. Light the candle and place it in front of the end of the can that has the small hole.

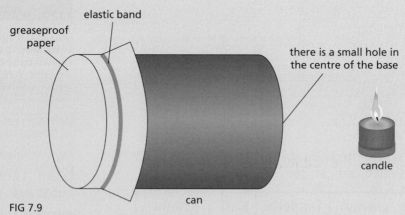

FIG 7.9

5. Look carefully at the image of the candle on the greaseproof paper at the other end of the can.
6. Draw the image exactly as you see it. (You may need to do this in a darkened room if it is a very bright day.)
7. Describe what is unusual about the image.
8. Explain why the image is this way.

The image of the **object**, in this case the candle, is **inverted** because light travels in straight lines.

Activity 7.3

Investigating the height of the image formed by a pinhole camera

Here is what you need:

- pinhole camera
- candle
- ruler.

Here is what you should do:

1. Place the lit candle 140 mm from the pinhole end of the camera.

⚠ **SAFETY**
Take care with a lit candle.

2. Measure the height of the image at the back of the camera.

3. Copy this table and write in the value.

Distance from the candle to the pinhole	Height of the image at the back of the camera
140 mm	
120 mm	
100 mm	
80 mm	
60 mm	

4. Repeat steps 1 to 3, placing the candle 120 mm, 100 mm, 80 mm and 60 mm from the pinhole. Enter your results in the table.

5. Describe what happens to the height of the image as the candle is brought nearer to the pinhole.

Check your understanding

1. Copy and complete the following sentences.

   a) Light only travels in _____ _____.

   b) A pinhole camera has no _____ but it can form an _____ on a screen.

   c) The image of a pinhole camera is _____.

   d) If the object in front of a pinhole camera is moved away from the pinhole it stays _____ but it becomes _____.

Fun fact

The famous Arabian scientist Ibn Al-Haythan (Alhazen) is credited with inventing the first pinhole camera over a thousand years ago.

Key terms

image picture of an object

object item pictured by the camera

inverted upside down

Transparent, translucent and opaque

We are learning how to:

- investigate the transmission of light in different media
- describe what happens when light strikes a material.

Transparent, translucent and opaque ⟫

When light strikes an object it is absorbed, reflected or refracted.

We can put materials into groups according to how much light they **absorb** and how much light passes through them.

A transparent material lets most of the light pass through it.

A translucent material absorbs some light and also lets some light pass through it.

An opaque material absorbs all the light and lets none pass through it.

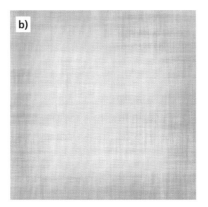
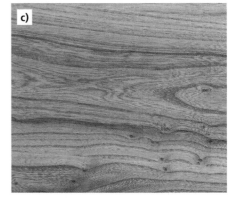

FIG 7.10 **a)** Glass is a transparent material

b) Cotton is a translucent material

c) Wood is an opaque material

Activity 7.4

Transparent, translucent and opaque materials

Here is what you need:

- different materials • torch • modelling clay.

Here is what you should do:

1. Place a torch on a book at one end of your table.

2. Look from the other end of the table.

3. Hold the material between the torch and your eye or stand it on the table using modelling clay.

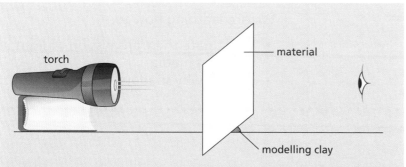

torch

material

modelling clay

FIG 7.11

4. Look at how much light is passing through the material. You must ignore any light shining on it from other sources.

5. Copy and complete the table to record what you have found by ticking the appropriate box for each material.

Name of material	Transparent	Translucent	Opaque

Check your understanding

1. **a)** Is this window best described as transparent, translucent or opaque?

   b) State two differences in the light passing out of the window compared with the light passing into the window.

FIG 7.12 This window is made of coloured glass

Key term
....

absorb take in

Shadows

We are learning how to:
- investigate the transmission of light in different media
- explain why shadows form.

Shadows 》》

An opaque object does not allow light to pass through it. Such an object casts a **shadow** on the side opposite from where it is illuminated. A shadow is a shape formed when the path of light is blocked by an opaque object.

FIG 7.14 Shadows form because light travels in straight lines (if light was able to bend around an object, the object would not cast a shadow)

Activity 7.5

Investigating shadows

Here is what you will need:

- torch with lens covered by a card with a hole in it
- cardboard star shape
- screen or area of lightly-coloured wall
- ruler
- modelling clay.

Here is what you should do:

1. Place a torch on some books a metre or so in front of a screen.

2. Fix a star shape 10 cm from the screen using modelling clay.

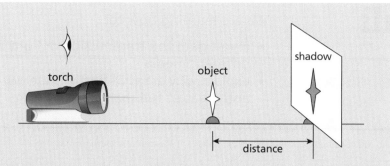

FIG 7.15

3. Measure the height of the star.

4. Repeat steps 2 and 3 four more times but moving the star away from the screen by an additional 10 cm each time.

5. Record the distance from the screen to the object and the height of the shadow each time in a table.

Check your understanding

1. Fig 7.16 shows an opaque object between a light source and a screen.

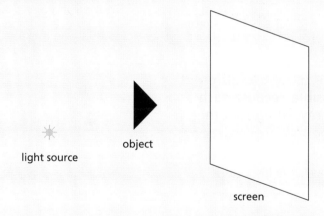

FIG 7.16

a) Copy Fig 7.16 and draw straight lines from the light source through the corners of the object to show the shadow that is formed on the screen.

b) State one similarity and one difference between the object and its shadow.

Fun fact

Shadow puppets are a popular form of entertainment in some parts of the world.

Some skilled artists are able to arrange their hands in such a way as to create shadows that resemble animals and other shapes.

Try some of these:

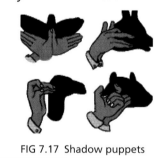

FIG 7.17 Shadow puppets

Key term

shadow a shape formed when the path of light is blocked by an opaque object

Partial and full shadow

We are learning how to:

- investigate the transmission of light in different media
- explain why areas of partial shadow and areas of full shadow may form.

Partial and full shadow

A **point light source** creates a single area of shadow behind the object.

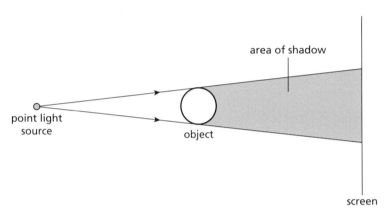

FIG 7.18 Shadow created by a point light source

When a large or **extended light source** is used, two different areas of shadow are created. This is possible because each side of the extended light source sends rays of light both above and below the object.

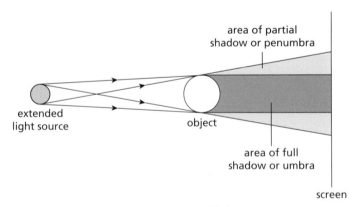

FIG 7.19 Shadow created by an extended light source

An area of full shadow, called the **umbra**, is created immediately behind the object. Surrounding the umbra there is an area of partial shadow called the **penumbra**.

Investigating the shadow formed by an extended light source

Here is what you need:

- torch
- cardboard circle shape
- screen or area of lightly-coloured wall
- ruler
- modelling clay.

Here is what you should do:

1. Place a torch on some books a metre or so in front of a screen.
2. Hold a circular shape about 10 cm from the screen.
3. Move the object back and forth until you can see an area of full shadow and an area of partial shadow surrounding it. Fix the object in place using modelling clay.

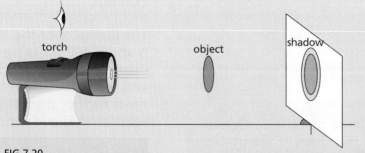

torch   object   shadow

FIG 7.20

4. Measure the diameter of the area of full shadow.
5. Measure the width of the band of partial shadow.
6. Make a labelled diagram of the shadow cast by the object.

Fun fact

Objects often cast areas of full and partial shadow when illuminated by everyday light sources such as lamps.

However, we are often not aware of them because the area of partial shadow appears as no more than a fuzzy border around the area of full shadow.

Check your understanding

1. A student is sitting under a small lamp. He is finding it difficult to read a book. Answer the following questions in terms of the shadows formed.

   a) Explain why, in terms of light and the formation of shadows, the student is finding it difficult to read.

   b) What difference would it make if the small lamp was replaced by a long fluorescent strip light?

FIG 7.21

Key terms

point light source source of light that creates a single area of shadow behind an object

extended light source source of light that creates two different areas of shadow

umbra area of full shadow

penumbra area of partial shadow

Solar eclipse

We are learning how to:

- investigate the transmission of light in different media
- explain why solar eclipses take place.

Solar eclipse >>>

The Sun acts as an extended source of light. The Earth orbits the Sun and the Moon orbits the Earth. Sometimes the Sun, the Earth and the Moon line up in a straight line.

A **solar eclipse** takes place when the Moon passes between the Sun and the Earth. The eclipse is the result of the shadow cast by the Moon passing over the Earth.

Activity 7.7

Modelling a solar eclipse

You should carry out this activity in a small group.

Here is what you need:

- torch
- large ball
- small ball
- marker.

The torch represents the Sun, the large ball the Earth and the small ball the Moon. Different members of the group will hold each one.

Here is what you should do:

1. Draw an 'X' on the large ball to represent the position of Trinidad and Tobago.

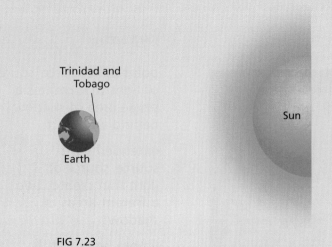

FIG 7.23

2. Place the Earth about 2 m from the Sun.
3. Bear in mind that the Moon is much nearer to the Earth than it is to the Sun.

Fun fact

The diameter of the Sun is about 400 times the diameter of the Moon and the Sun is about 400 times further from the Earth than the Moon.

FIG 7.22 The Sun and Moon appear to be similar in size when viewed from the Earth

This is why the Sun and the Moon look to be very similar in size when we see them in the sky.

Key term

solar eclipse when the Moon passes between the Sun and the Earth, the Moon casts a shadow as it passes across the Earth

4. Place the Moon in different positions between the Earth and the Sun until you find a place where the Moon casts a shadow on Trinidad and Tobago.

5. Redraw Fig 7.23 showing the position of the Moon.

During a solar eclipse the Moon passes in front of the Sun.

The Sun is so large compared to the Moon that the Moon casts a region of full shadow, called the umbra, and a region of partial shadow called the penumbra on the Earth.

What people see on Earth during a solar eclipse depends on where they are:

- people in the umbra will see a total eclipse

- people in the penumbra will see a partial eclipse

- people outside the penumbra will not see any eclipse.

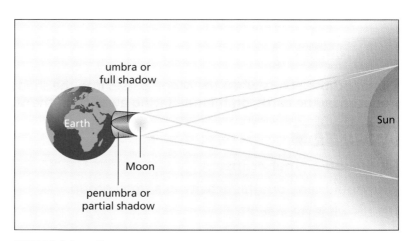

FIG 7.24 Solar eclipse

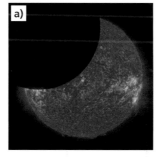 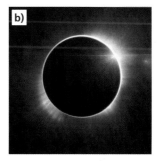

FIG 7.25 **a)** Partial eclipse of the Sun **b)** Total eclipse of the Sun

Check your understanding

1. Fig 7.26 shows the Sun, the Moon and the Earth.

FIG 7.26

a) Which eclipse takes place when the three bodies are in this position?

b) Copy and complete Fig 7.26 by drawing lines to show the shadow cast by the Moon on the Earth.

c) Label the umbra and the penumbra.

Lunar eclipse

We are learning how to:

- investigate the transmission of light in different media
- explain why lunar eclipses take place.

Lunar eclipse ⟫

A **lunar eclipse** occurs when the Moon passes into the shadow produced by the Earth, on the side facing away from the Sun.

Activity 7.8

Modelling a lunar eclipse

You should carry out this activity in a small group.

Here is what you need:

- torch
- large ball
- small ball
- marker.

The torch represents the Sun, the large ball the Earth and the small ball the Moon. Different members of the group will hold each one.

Here is what you should do:

1. Draw an 'X' on the large ball to represent the position of Trinidad and Tobago.

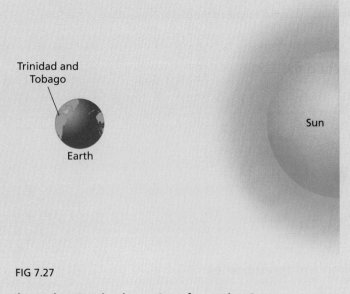

FIG 7.27

2. Place the Earth about 2 m from the Sun.

3. Bear in mind that the Moon is much nearer to the Earth than it is to the Sun.

Key term

lunar eclipse when the Moon passes into the shadow produced by the Earth

4. Place the Moon in different positions around the Earth until you find a place where the Moon is in the shadow of the Earth and could not be seen from Trinidad and Tobago.

5. Redraw Fig 7.27 showing the position of the Moon.

During a lunar eclipse the Moon passes into the Earth's shadow. As the Moon does not produce its own light, it looks even darker in the Earth's shadow during a lunar eclipse.

The Moon may pass through a region of partial or a region of full shadow:

- when the Moon passes through the Earth's penumbra we see a partial eclipse

- when the Moon passes through the Earth's umbra we see a total eclipse.

In fact, the Moon never becomes totally invisible. This is because some light is refracted towards it by the Earth's atmosphere. During a total lunar eclipse the Moon often looks red as a result of this refracted light.

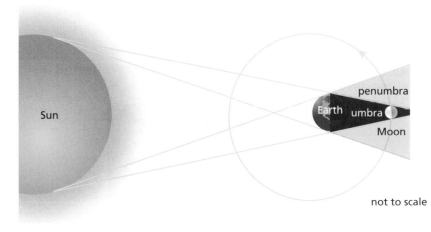

not to scale

FIG 7.28 Lunar eclipse

FIG 7.29 **a)** Partial eclipse of the Moon **b)** Total eclipse of the Moon

Check your understanding

1. **a)** Draw a diagram to show the positions of the Sun, Earth and Moon during a lunar eclipse.

   b) Explain why the appearance of the Moon, as seen from Earth, becomes much darker during a lunar eclipse.

Fun fact

Islamic astronomers living over a thousand years ago knew enough about the movement of the Earth and the Moon to be able to predict accurately when eclipses would happen.

Reflection

We are learning how to:

- investigate the transmission of light in different media
- explain how light is reflected by mirrors.

Reflection ▶▶▶

Most surfaces **reflect** some light. When light is reflected it changes direction.

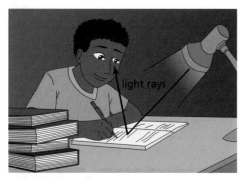

FIG 7.30 The reason people are able to see an object is because light is reflected off the object into their eyes

Activity 7.9

Measuring the angle of a reflected ray of light

Here is what you need:

- single beam light source
- ruler
- sheet of paper
- plane (flat) mirror
- protractor
- modelling clay.

Here is what you should do:

1. Draw a line along the long side of the paper a few centimetres in from the edge.

2. Place the protractor at the centre of the line and mark out the 180° in 10° divisions. Use your ruler to extend the lines. Don't forget to label them.

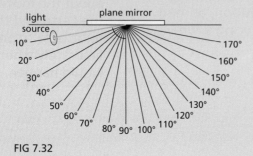

FIG 7.32

Fun fact

Emergency vehicles like ambulances have their names written back to front on the front of the vehicle. When the vehicle comes up behind another vehicle the driver will see the laterally inverted image in his mirror.

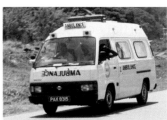

FIG 7.31 In the mirror image of this ambulance, the word 'AMBULANCE' will appear to be written the correct way around

Key terms

reflect light changes direction when it arrives at a reflecting surface

angle of incidence angle at which light arrives at a reflecting surface

angle of reflection angle at which light leaves a reflecting surface

lateral inversion when an image is formed in a plane mirror, the top and bottom remain the same but right and left change over

3. Place the mirror at the centre of the line using modelling clay to hold it.

4. The ray from the light source to the mirror is called the incident ray and the ray leaving the mirror is called the reflected ray.

5. Put the light source at an angle of 10° to the mirror and record the angle between the incident ray and the line at 90°.

6. Record the angle between the reflected ray and the line at 90°.

7. Repeat this for angles up to 90° in 10° intervals.

8. What is the relationship between the angles made by the incident ray and the reflected ray?

There are two laws of reflection.

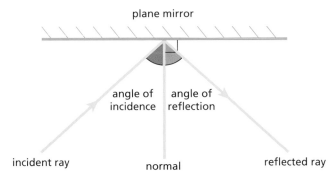

FIG 7.33 Ray of light reflected by a plane mirror

1. The **angle of incidence** equals the **angle of reflection**.

2. The incident ray, reflected ray and normal (a line perpendicular to the mirror) all lie in the same plane.

The reflection of an object is called its image. The image formed by a plane mirror looks identical to the object. However, it has one important difference. The man in figure 7.34 has the razor in his left hand but in the image it is in his right hand.

This effect is called **lateral inversion**.

FIG 7.34 Lateral inversion

Check your understanding

1. a) Draw a diagram to show a ray of light being reflected by a plane mirror.

   b) State a rule about the angle of incidence and the angle of reflection.

Refraction

We are learning how to:

- investigate the transmission of light in different media
- explain how light is refracted when it passes from one medium into another.

Refraction

The speed of light varies a little in different media. For example, it moves at slightly different speeds in air, in water and in glass. These materials each have a different **optical density** and **refractive index**.

When a ray of light passes from air into glass, the change of speed causes the ray to bend slightly towards the normal where it enters the glass. This bending of light is called **refraction**. As the ray leaves the glass it bends away from the normal by an equal amount. The only time that the ray of light is not refracted is if it enters the glass block at an angle of 90°, that is along the normal.

Activity 7.10

Measuring angle of incidence and angle of refraction

Here is what you need:

- single beam light source
- ruler
- sheet of paper
- glass block.
- protractor

Here is what you should do:

1. Place the glass block on the paper and draw around it.

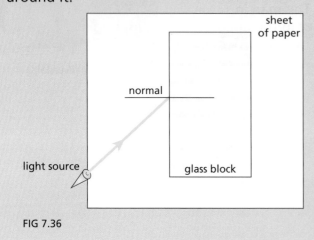

FIG 7.36

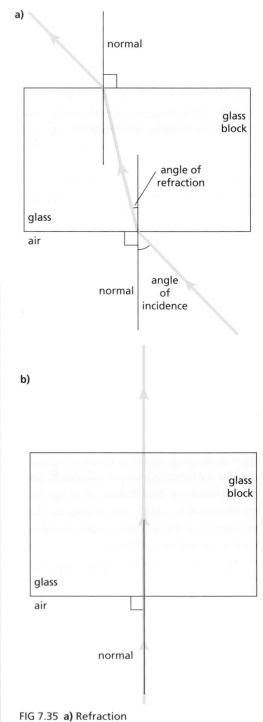

FIG 7.35 **a)** Refraction
b) Light entering the block of glass along the normal shows no refraction

2. Draw a normal to one of the long sides of the block.

3. Shine a ray of light at an angle to the glass block so it strikes the glass block at the normal.

4. Make a couple of marks along the ray of light and mark where the ray leaves the glass block.

5. Remove the glass block and draw in the incident ray and the refracted ray.

6. Mark and measure the angle of incidence and the angle of refraction.

Lenses are optical devices that cause rays of light to bend. Parallel rays of light either converge or diverge depending on the shape of the lens.

a)

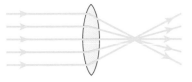

converging lens

b)

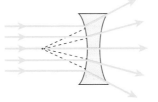

diverging lens

FIG 7.38 **a)** Converging lens **b)** Diverging lens

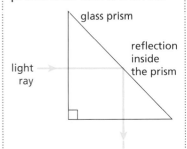
Check your understanding

1. Fig 7.39 shows a drinking straw in a glass of water.

   a) What is unusual about the appearance of the straw?

   b) Explain why it appears this way.

FIG 7.39

Key terms

optical density a measure of the extent to which a material transmits light

refractive index ratio of the speed of light in one medium compared to the speed of light in another medium

refraction bending of light as it travels from one medium to another

Real and apparent depth

We are learning how to:
- investigate the transmission of light in different media
- explain why objects under water appear nearer to the surface than they actually are.

Real and apparent depth ⟫⟫

Light is refracted when it passes between air and water. Objects in the water appear closer to the surface than they really are. If a coin is placed in a dish of water and viewed from the side, its **apparent depth** is less than its **real depth**.

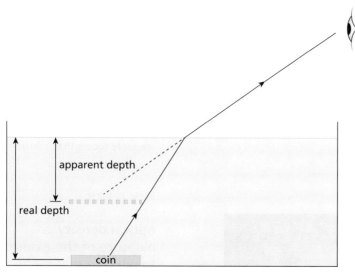

FIG 7.40 The light rays from the coin bend as they pass from water to air and make it look as though they are coming from a different place nearer the surface than they actually are

Activity 7.11

Investigating real and apparent depth

Here is what you need:

- glass block
- board
- two pins
- cork
- ruler.

Here is what you should do:

1. Place a glass block on a board.
2. Stick a pin at one end of the length of the glass block and observe it from the opposite end.

Key terms

apparent depth depth object appears to be at when viewed from above

real depth depth object actually is

3. Put a second pin in a piece of cork and place this on the block between you and the first pin so you cannot see the top of the first pin.

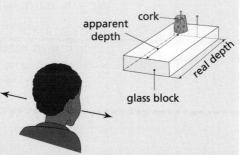

FIG 7.41

4. Move the cork along the glass block until the top of the second pin appears to sit on the bottom of the first pin and they remain the same, even when you move your head to the left and right.

5. Measure the distance from the front of the block to the first pin (real depth) and from the front of the glass block to the second pin (apparent depth).

The refractive index is the ratio of the speed of light in one medium compared with another. You can use the results of the activity to find the refractive index of glass/air using the equation:

$$\text{refractive index} = \frac{\text{real depth}}{\text{apparent depth}}$$

To spear a fish under water, a fisherman must aim a little below the fish and not directly at it.

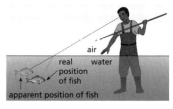

FIG 7.42

Light rays reflected by the fish are refracted as they pass from water into air. So, to the fisherman, the fish appears to be in a different position from where it really is.

Check your understanding

1. Light rays change direction as they leave a jar of water.

   a) What causes the light rays to change direction as they pass from water to air?

   b) A boy looks at the coin from above the jar of water. Show the position of the image of the coin and label it 'I'.

   c) Using a ruler measure:

   i) the distance from the surface of the water to I.

   ii) the distance from the surface of the water to the coin.

   d) The refractive index is the ratio of the speed of light in two different media such as water and air. Use the equation below to calculate this ratio for air and water.

   $$\text{refractive index} = \frac{\text{real depth}}{\text{apparent depth}}$$

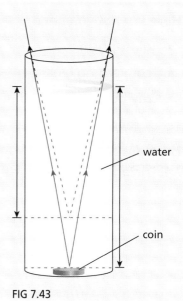

FIG 7.43

Dispersion

We are learning how to:

- investigate the transmission of light in different media
- describe how white light is dispersed as a result of refraction.

Dispersion >>>

The light we receive from the Sun is called **white light**. It is not a single colour but a mixture of many different colours.

Light is refracted when it passes from one medium into another. The different colours of light in white light are refracted by slightly different amounts when they pass between air and glass or plastic. This provides a way of separating them. This effect is called **dispersion**.

This is sometimes called a **visible spectrum**. Red light is refracted least while violet light is refracted most.

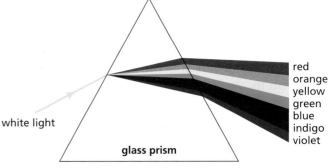

white light

glass prism

FIG 7.44 The result of dispersion is a spectrum of coloured light running from red through to violet

Activity 7.12

Creating a spectrum

Here is what you need:

- glass prism
- converging lens
- ray box or source of narrow beam of light
- screen.

Here is what you should do:

1. Arrange the apparatus as shown in Fig 7.45.

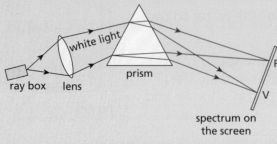

FIG 7.45

2. Move the screen and/or the lens until the colours of the spectrum do not overlap and a sharp image is formed.

If two prisms are placed in opposite orientations, the light that is separated into colours due to refraction by the first prism is refracted in the opposite way by the second.

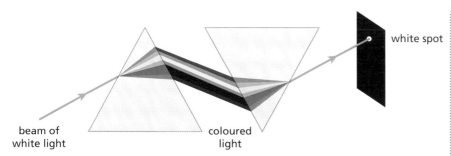

FIG 7.46 The result of putting white light through two prisms in opposite orientations is that the coloured lights recombine to form white light

Check your understanding

1. Fig 7.47 shows white light being separated into different colours.

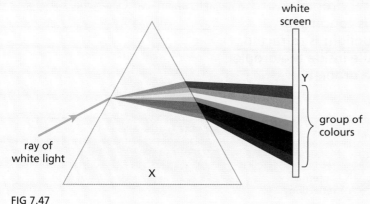

FIG 7.47

a) What is the name of:

i) the triangular piece of glass marked X?

ii) the group of coloured bands that appear on the screen?

iii) the process that separates white light into bands of different colours?

b) i) What colour appears at Y?

ii) Which colour of light is refracted the most?

Fun fact

Sir Isaac Newton is credited with first suggesting that sunlight is composed of lights of different colours. He identified seven colours: red, orange, yellow, green, blue, indigo and violet.

However, some scientists argue that Newton chose seven because it happened to coincide with the number of days in the week and the number of objects known in the Solar System at that time, and he thought that would make the result more important. They suggest that indigo should not be regarded as a colour in its own right but merely a shade of blue or violet, thus making only six colours.

Key terms

white light light that is not a single colour but a mixture of many different colours

dispersion separating white light into different colours

visible spectrum a group of different colours of light running from red through to violet

Rainbows

We are learning how to:

• investigate the transmission of light in different media
• explain the formation of rainbows.

Rainbows »

The visible spectrum obtained by the dispersion of white light might have reminded you of a rainbow.

When a rainbow is observed, the Sun is actually behind the observer, who is looking up at an angle of about 45° to the ground. Each droplet of water in the air acts like a tiny prism that both refracts and reflects the sunlight.

FIG 7.48 Rainbows form as a result of the refraction of sunlight by droplets of water in the atmosphere

There are many different paths that a ray of light can take as it passes through a water droplet. As far as the formation of a rainbow is concerned, the path needed is one in which sunlight is refracted entering the droplet, reflected while inside the droplet, and refracted again as it leaves the droplet.

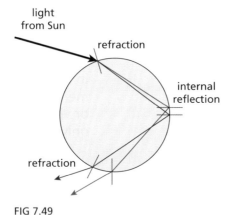

FIG 7.49

You generally see a rainbow as a circular arc across the sky. The colour bands begin at the top with red, followed by the other colours of the spectrum, ending in violet. The reason why red is at the top and violet is at the bottom is to do with the angles at which the different colours leave the water droplets.

Different bands of colour in a rainbow are formed by different bands of water droplets. Fig 7.50 shows only the water droplets at the top and at the bottom of a rainbow.

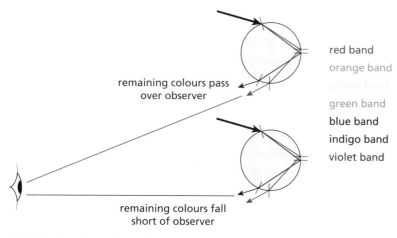

red band
orange band
yellow band
green band
blue band
indigo band
violet band

remaining colours pass over observer

remaining colours fall short of observer

FIG 7.50 Formation of a rainbow

At the top of the rainbow, the red light is refracted at a steep enough angle to pass to your eye. All the other colours from these droplets are refracted at shallower angles and pass over your head. At the bottom of the rainbow the violet light is refracted at a suitably shallow angle to reach your eye. The remaining colours from these droplets are refracted at steeper angles and fall to the ground in front of you.

Activity 7.13

Remembering the colours of the rainbow in order

You should work in a group for this activity. You will not need any equipment or materials.

A mnemonic is a device that helps you to remember something. Here is one example:

Mr Roy G Biv

The letters R-O-Y G B-I-V are the same as the first letter of each colour in the spectrum in the correct order.

Your task is to devise a similar mnemonic that will help you remember the colours of the rainbow in their correct order. It should be something that refers to Trinidad and Tobago or to the Caribbean.

Check your understanding

1. a) Draw a diagram to show how a rainbow would appear in the sky and label the red and violet parts.

    b) Suggest why rainbows are often seen after it has been raining.

Fun fact

Sometimes double rainbows appear when conditions are favourable.

FIG 7.51 Double rainbow

What do you notice about the order of the colours in the two parts of the rainbow?

Review of Light

- A beam of light consists of two or more light rays. Light rays can be:
  - parallel
  - converging to a point
  - diverging from a point.

- Light normally travels in straight lines. This is called rectilinear propagation.

- A pinhole camera is a simple optical device that contains no lens or photographic film. An image is formed at the rear of the camera.

- The image of a pinhole camera is always inverted. Its size depends on:
  - the distance between the object and the pinhole
  - the distance between the pinhole and the image.

- Materials can be classified as:
  - transparent if they allow most light to pass through them
  - translucent if they allow some light to pass through them
  - opaque if they do not allow any light to pass through them.

- A shadow is formed by an opaque object on the opposite side from a source of light that illuminates it. A shadow is an area that does not receive light. The formation of shadows is proof that light travels in straight lines.

- When an object is illuminated by an extended light source it forms:
  - an area of full shadow called the umbra
  - an area of partial shadow called the penumbra.

- A solar eclipse occurs when the Moon is positioned exactly between the Sun and the Earth.

- A lunar eclipse occurs when the Earth is positioned exactly between the Sun and the Moon.

- Solar eclipses and lunar eclipses may be full or partial depending on where they are viewed from on Earth.

- The reason why we can see objects is because they reflect light into our eyes. A light ray striking an object is called the incident ray, and the ray leaving an object is called the reflected ray.

- A normal is a line perpendicular to a reflecting surface such as a mirror. The angle made by the incident ray and the normal is called the angle of incidence. The angle made by the reflected ray and the normal is called the angle of reflection.

- The two laws of reflection are:

  1. angle of incidence = angle of reflection

  2. the incident ray, the normal and the reflected ray are all in the same plane.

- When a light ray passes from one medium into another, the speed of the ray changes by a small amount. This small change causes the light ray to bend or be refracted.

- The optical density of a substance is the amount it resists the passage of light rays through it. Different materials have different optical densities.

- The refraction of light passing from water to air causes objects in the water to appear closer to the surface than they actually are. An object has a real depth and an apparent depth.

- The refractive index is the ratio of the speed of light in one material compared with another. The refractive index for water/air can be found using the equation:

$$\text{refractive index} = \frac{\text{real depth}}{\text{apparent depth}}$$

- Sunlight can be described as white light. It is a mixture of different coloured lights. When sunlight passes through a glass prism it is dispersed. The different coloured lights are separated because they are all refracted by slightly different amounts.

- The dispersion of sunlight produces a spectrum containing seven different colours: red, orange, yellow, green, blue, indigo, violet.

- A rainbow is formed when tiny droplets of water in the atmosphere act like prisms and separate sunlight into bands of different colours.

Review questions on Light

1. A truck driver sees a fire engine in his wing mirror.

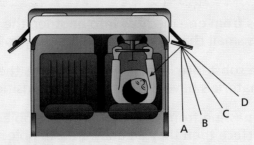

FIG 7.52

a) In which position, A, B, C or D, is the front of the fire engine?

b) The driver sees the word 'FIRE' in his mirror. How is the word written on the front of the fire engine?

2. Fig 7.53 shows a ray of light passing from air into a glass block.

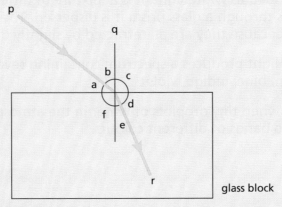

FIG 7.53

a) Which is the incident ray?

b) What name is given to line q?

c) Which of the angles marked are right angles?

d) Which is the:

   i) angle of refraction?

   ii) angle of incidence?

e) In what way would the diagram be different if it was drawn to show a light ray passing from the glass block into air?

3. **a)** What is the difference between an umbra and a penumbra?

   b) Copy and complete the following sentences using the words 'Earth' or 'Moon' in each gap.

   i) A lunar eclipse occurs when the _____ passes between the _____ and the Sun.

   ii) A solar eclipse occurs when the _____ passes between the Sun and the _____ .

   c) The Moon completes an orbit of the Earth every 28 days but we do not see a solar eclipse on the Earth every 28 days. Explain why.

4. A man has fitted a mirror at the end of his driveway so he can see what traffic is approaching as he drives out into the road. The driveway is at right angles to the road.

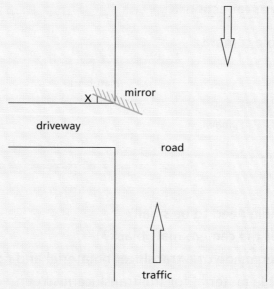

FIG 7.54

   a) Approximately what should the value of angle X be to give the man the best view down the road?

   b) A van comes up the road with the name 'BISWAS' written in large letters on the front of it. How would the name appear to the man sitting in his car in the driveway and looking at the mirror?

   c) What phrase describes the changes observed when an object is viewed in a plane mirror?

5. **a)** Explain the difference between a transparent, a translucent and an opaque material. Give one example of each type of material.

   b) Which type of material would be best for a bathroom window? Explain your answer.

6. Fig 7.55 shows a ray of light reflected by a plane mirror.

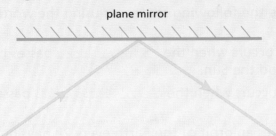

FIG 7.55

a) Redraw Fig 7.55, adding and labelling the normal, the angle of incidence and the angle of reflection.

b) State the two laws of reflection.

7. Fig 7.56 shows a pinhole camera.

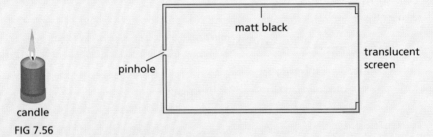

FIG 7.56

a) Why does the pinhole need to be small?

b) Why is the inside of the camera matt black?

c) i) Why is the screen made of a translucent material and not an opaque material?

   ii) Suggest a suitable material for the translucent screen.

d) Draw the image as it would appear on the screen.

e) How would the image change, if at all, if the candle was moved closer to the pinhole?

8. a) Explain the difference between a partial solar eclipse and a total solar eclipse.

b) With the help of a suitable diagram, explain how it is possible for people at different locations on the Earth so see a full solar eclipse, a partial solar eclipse or no solar eclipse at the same time.

9. a) What is the process in which white light is separated into light of different colours when passed through a glass prism?

b) Why does this separation take place?

c) Give the names of the different coloured lights in order, starting with red.

d) Briefly explain how rain droplets in the atmosphere are responsible for producing a rainbow.

10. Fig 7.57 shows a ray of light hitting a glass block.

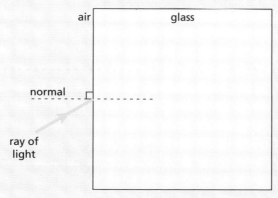

FIG 7.57

a) Copy Fig 7.57 and then:

  i) show the path of the ray through the block and out into the air

  ii) mark the angle of incidence (i) and the angle of refraction (r) where the light ray enters the block.

b) At the point where the light ray leaves the glass block, is the angle of incidence less than, the same as or greater than the angle of refraction?

c) In an activity, a student shone a ray of light into the glass block at different angles of incidence and measured the angle of refraction each time. The results are given in the table.

Angle of incidence	Angle of refraction
0°	0°
15°	10°
30°	19°
45°	28°
60°	35°
75°	40°

TABLE 7.1

  i) Draw a graph of angle of incidence against angle of refraction.

  ii) Are the angle of incidence and the angle of refraction always in the same ratio? How can you tell this from your graph?

  iii) Use your graph to estimate the angle of refraction when the angle of incidence is 50°.

  iv) At what angle of incidence is the ray of light not refracted?

  v) What happens to a ray of light striking the glass block at this angle?

Unit 8: Chemical bonding

Chemical bonding ▶▶

Electron configuration

For the first 20 elements, the maximum number of electrons for each shell is as follows:

1st shell – 2

2nd shell – 8

3rd shell – 8

The atoms of helium, neon and argon have a full outer shell. This is called full electron configuration because they have the maximum number of electrons in all of their electron shells. Atoms with full electron configuration are stable.

FIG 8.1 Uses of **a)** helium **b)** neon and **c)** argon

Chemical bonding

Atoms of the other elements have unstable electron configurations. Atoms of elements combine in different ways to form stable molecules.

FIG 8.2 The chemical name of table salt is sodium chloride and it is made from two elements, sodium and chlorine

Sodium and chlorine bond together by a process called ionic bonding.

Water is the result of bonding hydrogen with oxygen, although its name gives no hint about the atoms it is composed of. The bonding between hydrogen and oxygen in water is a different type of bonding from that between sodium and chlorine in table salt.

Oxygen is the gas that we breathe and it takes two atoms to bond to give us the air that we need for survival.

FIG 8.3 Bonding in metals is another type of bonding

The atoms in pure metal elements are also bonded together, but in a different way called metallic bonding.

In this unit, you will learn about the different types of chemical bonding.

Formation of ions

We are learning how to:

- explain how ionic bonding occurs
- illustrate how transfer of electrons occurs when the number of electrons gained by one atom is the same as the number of electrons lost by the other.

Gaining and losing the same number of electrons ⟩⟩

If the outermost shell of an atom does not contain as many electrons as it can, then the atom will combine with other atoms. The outermost shell is therefore the one that we need to look at when we talk about different types of bonding.

Activity 8.1

Ionic bonding

In this activity you will be exploring the bonding that forms kitchen salt. You will use bangles to represent the outermost shell of each atom.

Here is what you need:

- bangles
- modelling clay in two colours.

Here is what you should do:

1. Use one colour of modelling clay to create the electrons for the outer shell of the sodium atom and the other colour to create the electrons for the outer shell of the chlorine atom.

2. How many does each shell need to be stable?

3. Suggest what could be done for each atom to be stable.

4. If sodium loses the electron in its outer shell, would it lose that shell also?

5. So which shell would be the outermost? How many electrons are there in that shell?

6. Since an atom is satisfied when the last shell is filled, can we say that both sodium and chlorine are satisfied?

7. Draw the electron configuration of a sodium atom and a chlorine atom and explain what happens when bonding occurs.

The bonding of sodium and chlorine is called **ionic bonding**. The electron on the outermost shell of the sodium atom is transferred to the outer shell of chlorine. This means that, as sodium loses an electron, chlorine gains the electron. Sodium also loses that outer (valence) shell. Its second shell, containing eight electrons, now becomes its outermost.

With eight electrons on the outermost shell, both sodium and chlorine will have full outer shells. They have formed stable ions. An ion is a particle with fewer or more electrons than the neutral atom. The bonding is termed ionic because it involves the transfer of electrons and the formation of ions. The new substance is called a compound.

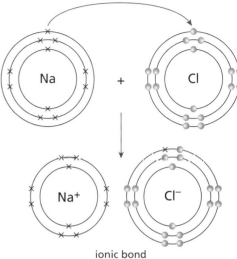

ionic bond

FIG 8.4 Ionic bonding of sodium chloride

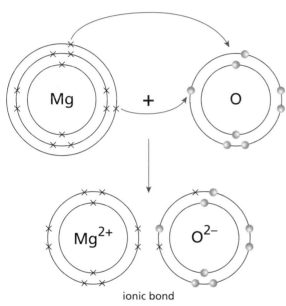

ionic bond

FIG 8.5 In the bonding of magnesium and oxygen, two electrons of magnesium are transferred to oxygen so, as magnesium loses two electrons, oxygen gains two electrons and both magnesium and oxygen become stable

Fun fact

Ionic bonding cannot occur between two metals.

Key terms

ionic bonding bonding where electrons on the outermost shell of one atom are transferred to the outer shell of another atom

stable atoms atoms that have a full outer shell of electrons

Check your understanding

1. Follow the steps in the activity above to bond these:

   a) potassium (2, 8, 8, 1) and fluorine (2, 7)
   b) magnesium (2, 8, 2) and oxygen (2, 6)
   c) calcium (2, 8, 8, 2) and sulfur (2, 8, 6)

Formation of ions 2

We are learning how to:

- explain how atoms become ions
- write the ions in chemical bonding
- give the name of a compound.

The formation of ions >>>

Atoms forming ions may lose one, two or more electrons. Other atoms can gain one, two or more electrons.

Activity 8.2

The charges on ions

Here is what you need:

Diagrams of ionic bonding that you completed in the previous lessons.

Here is what you should do:

1. On the left-hand side of your notebook page, draw the nucleus of a sodium atom with a diameter of about 2 cm.

2. Use ⊕ to represent each proton in the nucleus.

3. Use ⊖ to represent each electron and complete the configuration.

4. In the same way, draw an atom of chlorine next to sodium. Is each atom neutral? Why?

5. Below your diagrams, draw how bonding occurs.

6. Write the numbers of protons and electrons that are in each atom.

7. Are the numbers of protons and electrons equal as they were before?

8. Do you think that sodium and chlorine are still neutral?

9. Which charge would you give to each one? Why?

When an atom loses electrons, the number of protons becomes greater than the number of remaining electrons. The new resulting particle is positively charged and is called a positively charged ion. Conversely, when an atom gains electrons, it becomes negatively charged as the number of electrons is greater than the number of protons. The new particle is called a negatively charged ion.

The bonding of sodium with chlorine forms an Na⁺ ion and a Cl⁻ ion.

Naming compounds

To name a compound, the positively charged ion is normally written first. So, the compound formed from sodium and chlorine is sodium chloride, NaCl. The charges are not included in the name because in bonding the charges cancel each other out.

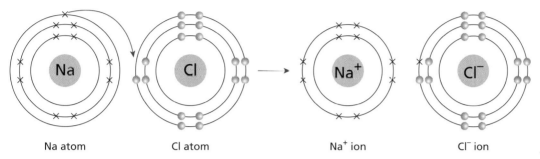

FIG 8.6 Sodium and chloride ions forming sodium chloride

Na atom   Cl atom   Na⁺ ion   Cl⁻ ion

What happens when the loss or gain is two?

When magnesium bonds with oxygen, each atom of magnesium loses two electrons. The number of protons is two more than the number of electrons and it becomes an Mg^{2+} ion. Also, each atom of oxygen gains two electrons and it becomes an O^{2-} ion. The compound formed is MgO. When the name of a compound is written using symbols, it is referred to as a **chemical formula** because more than one chemical symbol is written.

> **Fun fact**
>
> In chlorinated swimming pools, positively charged copper ions interact with negatively charged hair to make blonde hair turn green.

Check your understanding

1. Follow the steps in the activity to form ions and then the compound from:

   a) potassium (2, 8, 8, 1) and fluorine (2, 7).

   b) lithium (2, 1) and chlorine (2, 8, 7).

2. Show the compound formed when calcium (2, 8, 2) and sulfur (2, 8, 6) bond.

Key terms

ion a particle that has an electric charge

chemical formula the name of a compound written using symbols

Gaining and losing different numbers of electrons

We are learning how to:

- describe ionic bonding
- illustrate how the transfer of electrons occurs when the number of electrons gained by one atom and the number of electrons lost by the other atom are different.

Gaining and losing different numbers of electrons ▶▶▶

Activity 8.3

Ionic bonding

In this activity, you will be exploring the bonding of sodium oxide, a chemical used to make glass. You will again use bangles to represent the outermost shell of the atoms.

Here is what you need:

- bangles
- modelling clay in two colours.

Here is what you should do:

1. Use one colour of modelling clay to create the outer electron for the sodium atom and another colour to create the outer electrons for the oxygen atom.

2. How many does each shell need to be stable?

3. Look at the shells and suggest what should be done so that each atom would be stable.

4. If sodium loses its one electron, will oxygen gain it?

5. Will both sodium and oxygen then have full electron configuration?

6. How many electrons does oxygen still need?

7. Would another sodium atom be needed to give oxygen a full electron configuration?

8. Draw the electron configuration of sodium and oxygen atoms.

9. Show what happens when bonding occurs.

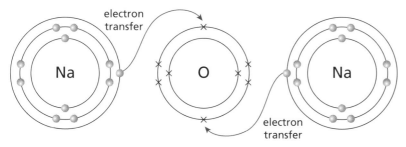

FIG 8.7 When sodium and oxygen bond, the electron on the outermost shell of the sodium atom is transferred to the outer shell of oxygen, but oxygen needs two electrons to become stable, so it takes two sodium atoms to fill the outer shell of one oxygen atom

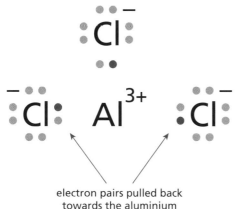

electron pairs pulled back towards the aluminium

FIG 8.8 Aluminium (2, 8, 3) needs three chlorine (2, 8, 7) atoms to become stable

The number of atoms taking part in ionic bonding depends on:

- the number of electrons to be lost from one atom
- the number of electrons to be gained by one atom.

Ionic bonding occurs when the number of electrons in the valence shell is lower than four. These electrons are gained by atoms that have more than four electrons in their valence shell.

Check your understanding

1. Follow the steps in the activity to bond these:

    a) lithium (2, 1) and oxygen (2, 6)
    b) magnesium (2, 8, 2) and chlorine (2, 8, 7)

> **Fun fact**
>
> Ionic compounds often form crystalline solids. Sodium chloride is an example.
>
>
>
> FIG 8.9 Sodium chloride crystals

Ions where electron loss and gain are different

We are learning how to:

- describe how atoms combine to form molecules
- write the ions in chemical bonding where the numbers of electrons lost and gained are different
- write the compound formed where the numbers of electrons lost and gained are different.

Ions where electron loss and gain are different ≫

Activity 8.4

Bonding of lithium and oxygen

Here is what you need:

All the diagrams of ionic bonding that you completed in the previous lessons – you may need to refer to them.

Here is what you should do:

1. On the left-hand side of your notebook page, draw a lithium atom (2, 1) showing its electrons.

2. On the right, draw an oxygen atom (2, 6) showing its electrons.

3. Is each atom that you have drawn neutral?

4. How many electrons does lithium need to lose?

5. How many electrons does oxygen need?

6. How many lithium atoms are needed to make one oxygen atom stable?

7. Suggest how the formula for the compound should be written.

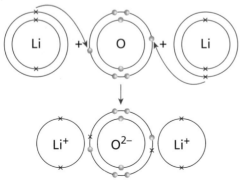

FIG 8.10 When lithium and oxygen bond, two lithium atoms are needed to satisfy one oxygen atom so the formula for the compound formed is Li_2O.

The number 2 in the formula Li_2O is called a subscript and is placed after the atom symbol. It shows the number of atoms of that element required to form the compound.

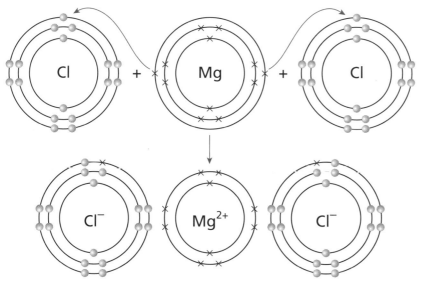

FIG 8.11 When magnesium bonds with chlorine, two chlorine atoms are needed to satisfy a magnesium atom so the formula for the compound formed is $MgCl_2$ (the subscript 2 is placed after the Cl symbol to indicate the number of ions of chlorine that have an equal and opposite charge to the magnesium ion)

FIG 8.12 Crystals of magnesium chloride

Check your understanding

1. Show the compound formed when the following pairs of atoms bond:

   a) calcium (2, 8, 8, 2) and chlorine (2, 8, 7)

   b) potassium (2, 8, 1) and sulfur (2, 8, 6)

2. What would the formula of an ionic compound of aluminium and fluorine be? Draw an electron structure for it similar to the one in Fig 8.11.

> **Fun fact**
>
> When ionic compounds dissolve in water, they become able to conduct electricity.

Valency

We are learning how to:

- describe how atoms combine to form molecules
- use the charge of an atom to write its formula.

Valency 》》

Activity 8.5

How charges help with writing formulae

Here is what you need:

Work completed in the previous lesson.

Here is what you should do:

1. Write each of the following pairs of atoms, allowing some space between the two symbols in each pair. Leave three lines between each pair.

   a) K + O   **b)** Mg + O   **c)** Li + O
   d) Mg + Cl   **e)** Al + F   **f)** Al + O

2. Write the charge that each atom has when it becomes an ion as a superscript (e.g. K^+ and O^{2-}).

3. Look at **a)**. Draw an arrow from the superscript of K to where the subscript of O should be placed.

4. In the same way, draw an arrow from the superscript of O to where the subscript of K should be placed.

5. On the next line, write the formula for K and O with the numbers in the positions shown by the arrows.

6. Compare the result with the answer you had from the previous lesson. Are they the same?

7. Follow steps 3 to 6 to complete **b)** to **f)**.

The method of switching charges is called the valence or crisscross method.

The lithium ion is written as Li^+ and the oxygen as O^{2-} indicating that Li loses one electron and O gains two. The charge that each ion carries is called its **valency**.

The formula for the compound formed when lithium combines with oxygen is written Li_2O since it takes two lithium atoms to satisfy one oxygen atom.

This is how the valence or crisscross method works.

$$\text{Li}^+ + \text{O}^{2-} \rightarrow \text{Li}_2\text{O}$$

$$\text{Na}^+ + \text{Cl}^- \rightarrow \text{NaCl}$$

FIG 8.13 How the valence or crisscross method works

Three points to remember when using the valence or crisscross method:

- when the subscript is 1, it is not necessary to write it

- when both subscripts are the same, it is not necessary to write them

- when the formula is written, the charges disappear because bonding occurs between an equal number of positive and negative charges, each cancelling out the other.

The advantage of this method is that, as long as you know the valence of the ions, it is easy to write a formula simply by crisscrossing the value of charges.

Check your understanding

1. Use the valence method to show the result of the bonding between the following pairs of atoms:

   a) Mg (2, 8, 2) + Cl (2, 8, 7)

   b) Na (2, 8, 1) + S (2, 8, 6)

   c) Ca (2, 8, 8, 2) + Cl (2, 8, 7)

   d) Na (2, 8, 1) + O (2, 6)

   e) Mg (2, 8, 2) + F (2, 7)

Key term
....

valency charge that each ion carries

Different atoms sharing electrons

We are learning how to:

- describe how atoms combine to form molecules
- illustrate covalent bonding in atoms of different types
- write the chemical formula representing the bonding.

Different atoms sharing electrons >>>

Covalent bonding occurs mostly between two non-metals. It is a method of bonding that involves sharing electrons in order to achieve full outer electron shells.

Activity 8.6

Exploring covalent bonding between hydrogen and oxygen to form water

Here is what you need:

- bangles
- modelling clay in two colours.

Here is what you should do:

1. Use one colour of modelling clay to create the electrons for the oxygen outer shell (oxygen is 2, 6) and use the other colour to create the electrons for the outer shell of hydrogen (hydrogen is 1).

2. What is the maximum number of electrons that each shell can hold?

3. Bring the two shells together so that one electron of each colour is shared. Is the hydrogen satisfied?

4. Is the oxygen satisfied?

5. What should be done to satisfy the oxygen? Go ahead and do it.

6. Are all three atoms now satisfied?

7. Using the symbols of the atoms, write the chemical formula for the bonding.

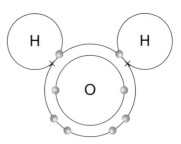

FIG 8.14 Covalent bonding of oxygen and hydrogen to form water

The maximum number of electrons that the only shell of hydrogen can hold is two. Hydrogen's shell, therefore, needs one more electron and oxygen's shell needs two. Hydrogen shares its one electron with one of oxygen, and is satisfied. Oxygen still requires one more. Another hydrogen atom is needed. The formula for the compound formed is H_2O. This is called a molecule of water.

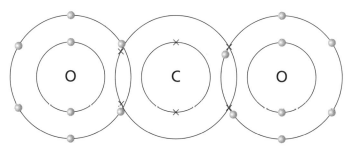

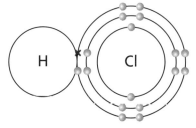

FIG 8.15 **a)** Carbon and oxygen can combine to form a molecule of CO_2

b) Hydrogen and chlorine can combine to form a molecule of HCl

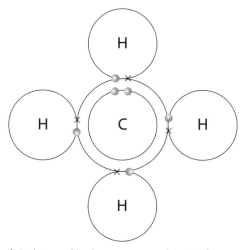

c) Carbon and hydrogen can combine to form a molecule of CH_4

When writing formulae with atoms from different groups, the atom from the lower group is normally written first. Because of the nature of hydrogen, its position in the formula may vary.

Check your understanding

1. Use the steps in the activity to form molecules with the following pairs of atoms:

   a) carbon and oxygen

   b) hydrogen and chlorine

   c) carbon and hydrogen

> **Fun fact**
>
> Covalent bonding involves strong connections between the atoms, so it is difficult to break these molecules apart.

Key term

covalent bonding bonding in which electrons are shared between atoms

Diatomic molecules

We are learning how to:

- describe how atoms combine to form molecules
- illustrate covalent bonding of atoms in diatomic molecules
- write the chemical equation representing the bonding.

Diatomic molecules 》》

In a covalent bond, the positively charged nuclei of both atoms are attracted by the oppositely charged electrons in the bond between them.

Activity 8.7

Covalent bonding of hydrogen

Here is what you need:

- bangles
- modelling clay.

Here is what you should do:

1. Make a representation of the outer shell of a hydrogen atom.

2. What is the maximum number of electrons that this shell can hold?

3. Make another representation of the outer shell of a hydrogen atom.

4. Show how you can use covalent bonding to satisfy the two hydrogen atoms.

5. How is a molecule of hydrogen gas written?

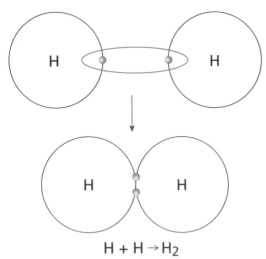

$H + H \rightarrow H_2$

FIG 8.16 The bonding of hydrogen atoms to form a hydrogen molecule

There is only one electron in a hydrogen atom's single shell. This makes the atom unstable since it does not have full electron configuration. When another hydrogen atom bonds with it, they each share their electrons (they are covalently bonded) and become stable. The molecule formed is hydrogen gas. This is written in symbols as H_2.

Since the molecule is made of two atoms, it is referred to as a **diatomic molecule**.

Activity 8.8

Forming other diatomic molecules

Here is what you need:

- bangles
- modelling clay.

Here is what you should do:

Use the bangles and modelling clay to represent the outermost shells of:

a) chlorine (2, 8, 7) **b)** fluorine (2, 7) **c)** oxygen (2, 6).

Follow the steps in Activity 8.7 to form diatomic molecules for each molecule.

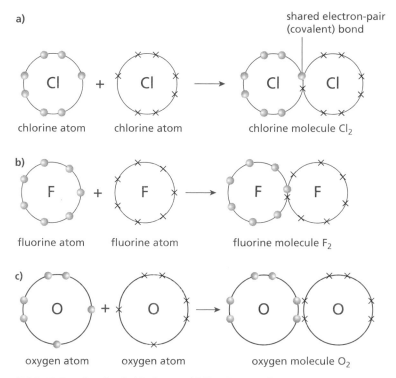

FIG 8.17 Bonding in **a)** chlorine gas **b)** fluorine gas **c)** oxygen gas

Check your understanding

1. Explain how covalent bonding is used to form diatomic molecules.

Key term

diatomic molecule a molecule consisting of two atoms

Metallic bonding

We are learning how to:

- describe metallic bonding.

Metallic bonding >>>

Activity 8.9

Thermal conductivity

This is a demonstration activity. You are to observe only.

Here is what you need:

- thumb tacks
- metal rod
- candle
- Bunsen burner.

Here is what you should do:

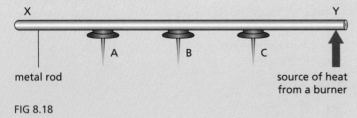

FIG 8.18

1. Attach three thumb tacks to a metal rod using candle wax.

2. Heat one end of the rod using a Bunsen burner.

3. Is the entire rod in contact with the flame of the burner?

4. What happens to tack C after about two minutes? Are B and A affected?

5. Do they eventually get affected? Why?

Metals are good conductors of heat, as we have seen in Activity 8.9. This is because of the way that metal atoms are bound together by metallic bonding.

For a similar reason, metals are generally good conductors of electricity. Now carry out Activity 8.10.

Activity 8.10

Electrical conductivity

Here is what you need:

- circuit wire
- cell
- selection of materials – conductors and insulators
- lamp.

Here is what you should do:

1. Use each of the materials to connect the two open ends of the electrical circuit.

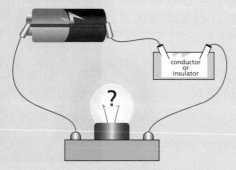

FIG 8.19

2. Did the bulb light with every material connected in the circuit? Why?

Metallic bonding does not involve losing, gaining or sharing of electrons. Metals have few electrons in their outermost shell. These electrons have the ability to move around freely. When one part of a metal is in contact with heat or electricity, the 'free electrons' in the contact area move around and transfer heat and electricity through the metal.

Metallic bonding is defined as the bonding occurring between atoms within metals because of the movement of free electrons through the arrangement of particles. The structure of any substance is dependent on the formation of its bonds.

Non-metals do not generally transfer heat and electricity easily because their atoms do not have free electrons.

Check your understanding

1. Explain why metals conduct heat and electricity but non-metals do not.

> **Fun fact**
>
> Metallic bonding also makes metals malleable: their shape can be changed by physical force.
>
> If a matchbox were filled with gold it could be flattened to make a sheet the size of a lawn tennis court.

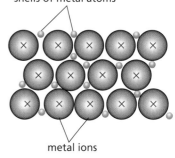

free electrons from outer shells of metal atoms

metal ions

FIG 8.20 Metallic bonding

Key term

metallic bonding the bonding occurring between atoms within metals because of the movement of free electrons through the arrangement of particles

Bonding and physical properties

The type of bonding in a substance is important in determining its physical properties.

Metals ▶▶▶

Metals generally have high **melting points** because a lot of energy is needed to overcome the attractive forces between the positive ions and the negative electrons.

The temperature of the filament in a traditional lamp is around 2500 °C when switched on. It is made of a metal called tungsten which has a melting point of 3422 °C.

Ionic compounds

Ionic compounds consist of a matrix of positively charged and negatively charged ions.

In sodium chloride, the forces of attraction between the positively charged sodium ions and the negatively charged chloride ions are very strong. In general, ionic compounds have high melting points.

Ionic compounds can carry an electric current when the ions are free to move. This is not possible when solid, but when an ionic compound is molten or dissolved in water the ions are free to move.

Simple covalent compounds

Covalent compounds can be classified as simple molecules or macromolecules. Methane, CH_4, is an example of a simple covalent compound.

The covalent bonds between the atoms in a molecule of methane are strong but the bonding between molecules is weak. Simple covalent compounds have low melting and boiling points. Many are gases even at room temperature.

Because covalent compounds do not contain free electrons or ions they cannot conduct electricity.

Giant covalent compounds

Some covalent compounds have a giant structure in which the same unit is repeated many times.

FIG 8.21 Tungsten filament lamp

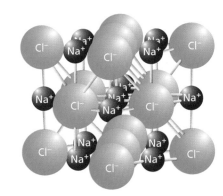

FIG 8.23 Sodium chloride

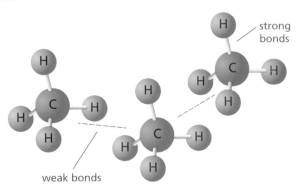

strong bonds

weak bonds

FIG 8.22 Methane

For example, silica consists of a matrix in which each silicon atom is bonded to four different oxygen atoms, and each oxygen atom is bonded to two different silicon atoms.

In order to melt, a very large amount of energy is needed to break the covalent bonds. Giant covalent structures are generally hard and have very high melting points.

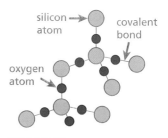

FIG 8.24 Silica

Activity 8.11

Investigating the properties of two compounds

Here is what you will need:

- glucose
- sodium chloride
- two hard glass test tubes
- test tube holder
- heat source
- two beakers 100 cm^3
- stirring rod
- circuit to test conductivity (battery, lamp and wires).

Here is what you should do:

1. Put a small amount of glucose in a hard glass test tube and heat it gently at first to see if it melts. If it doesn't melt, heat it more strongly. Record your observations.
2. Repeat step 1 using sodium chloride in place of glucose.
3. Put about 5 g of glucose in a beaker containing 50 cm^3 of water. Stir the solid until it dissolves.
4. Test whether the glucose solution conducts electricity using a suitable circuit. Record your observations.
5. Repeat steps 3 and 4 using sodium chloride in place of glucose.

Check your understanding

1.

Substance	Melting point and boiling point	Conducts electricity when solid	Conducts electricity when molten
A	Low	No	No
B	High	No	Yes
C	Very high	No	No
D	High	Yes	Yes

TABLE 8.1

Which of the substances in Table 8.1 is most likely to be:

a) a giant covalent compound; b) a metal;

c) an ionic compound; d) a simple covalent compound?

Key term

electron negatively charged particle

ion particle that may carry a positive or a negative charge

melting point temperature at which a solid becomes a liquid

ionic compound has bonds between oppositely charged ions

covalent compound has bonds in which electrons are shared

Review of Chemical bonding

- When atoms are attracted to each other, chemical bonding occurs.

- Bonding occurs so that the outermost shell of an atom is filled, forming a stable electron configuration.

- All atoms are neutral.

- When writing formulae, the atom losing electrons is usually written first.

- Atoms losing electrons become positively charged ions and those gaining electrons become negative ions.

- The valence or valency of an ion depends on the number of electrons it gains or loses.

- The valence or crisscross method helps to derive the formula of the products of a reaction.

- Covalent bonding occurs when electrons are shared between atoms.

- In ionic bonding, electrons are transferred from one atom to another.

- Covalent bonding occurs between atoms of Groups 4, 5, 6 and 7.

- Diatomic molecules are composed of two atoms.

- Diatomic molecules are covalent.

- The type of bonding in a substance influences its physical properties.

- Metals generally have high melting points and all metals are good conductors or heat and electricity.

- Ionic compounds generally have high melting points and conduct electricity when molten or dissolved in water.

- Simple covalent compounds have very low melting points and boiling points and many are gases at room temperature.

- Giant covalent compounds are hard and have very high melting points.

- Covalent compounds do not conduct electricity.

Review questions on Chemical bonding

1. Define the following terms:

   a) bonding   **b)** chemical formula.

2. Explain the difference between covalent and ionic bonding.

3. **a)** Name a diatomic gas.

   b) Show how that diatomic gas is made.

4. Using any method you know, write the chemical formula for the compound between the following:

   a) hydrogen (1) and fluorine (2, 7)

   b) sulfur (2, 8, 6) and chlorine (2, 8, 7)

   c) aluminium (2, 8, 3) and oxygen (2, 6)

   d) magnesium (2, 8, 2) and fluorine (2, 7)

   e) sodium (2, 8, 1) and oxygen (2, 6)

   f) calcium (2, 8, 8, 2) and oxygen (2, 6)

5. Indicate whether each of the following is true or false.

   a) Some ions have no electric charge.

   b) Calcium loses electrons so it carries a 2+ charge.

   c) Chlorine has seven valence electrons. It forms a Cl^- ion.

   d) Al^{3+} and F^- bond to form Al_3F.

   e) It is usual for metals to form positive ions.

   f) Methane, CH_4, is a highly acidic substance.

   g) Atoms like magnesium in Group 2 form ions with a 2– charge.

   h) Ionic substances usually share their unpaired electrons.

   i) Table salt, NaCl, is formed by ionic bonding.

Unit 9: Acids and alkalis

Acids and alkalis ⟫

One way of classifying matter is into acids and alkalis. Acids and alkalis are found in a wide variety of products.

a)

b)

FIG 9.1 **a)** Fruit contains acid

b) Baking soda is an alkali

FIG 9.2 These household chemicals may be acids or alkalis and many of them are corrosive

Many acids and alkalis may be hazardous.

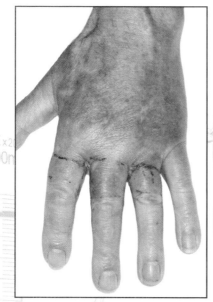

FIG 9.3 The effects of contact with sulfuric acid

The picture shows some of the effects of contact with sulfuric acid.

Calcium hydroxide is a mildly corrosive alkali. However, the product of the reaction of calcium hydroxide and sulfuric acid is calcium sulfate, which is a useful substance – it is used to make casts for supporting fractured bones.

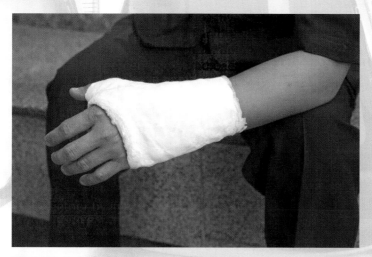

FIG 9.4 Calcium sulfate is used to make casts for supporting fractured bones

In this section you will be exploring how to distinguish between acids and alkalis. You will also learn about some reactions of acids.

Identifying acids

We are learning how to:

- distinguish between substances that are acids and alkalis
- explain the use of an indicator
- give the colour change in an indicator when it contacts an acid.

Identifying acids ⟩⟩⟩

Activity 9.1

Exploring how indicators change colour with different acids

Here is what you need:

- hydrochloric acid
- sulfuric acid
- nitric acid
- red and blue litmus paper

- phenolphthalein
- methyl orange
- test tubes
- tweezers
- droppers.

⚠️ **SAFETY**

Observe the safety icon on the acid bottles. All indicator papers should be held with tweezers. Avoid spillage.

Here is what you should do:

1. Copy the table.

Acid	Indicator	Colour change
hydrochloric (HCl) sulfuric (H_2SO_4) nitric (HNO_3)	red litmus paper	
hydrochloric sulfuric nitric	blue litmus paper	
hydrochloric sulfuric nitric	phenolphthalein	
hydrochloric sulfuric nitric	methyl orange	

2. Pour a few drops of hydrochloric acid into each of two test tubes.

3. Suck up a dropperful of hydrochloric acid from one of the test tubes.

4. Squeeze one drop of hydrochloric acid onto a piece of each of the coloured indicator papers and record the colour you observe.

5. Pour one drop of the liquid indicators into each of the two test tubes of hydrochloric acid. Record the colour change you observe.

6. Wash out all the test tubes and droppers thoroughly.

7. Repeat steps 2 to 6 for sulfuric acid and then for nitric acid.

8. Compare the results you found for the various acids. Did all acids give the same results for each indicator?

The word **acid** is from the Latin *acidus*, meaning sour. An acid is a chemical substance. Solutions formed from these chemical substances usually have a sour taste. In order to identify acids, **indicators** are used. Indicators are made from special dyes and the results of your experiments should show the colour change.

Activity 9.2

Check your breath

In this activity you will explore the gas that is exhaled from your body.

Here is what you need:

- two test tubes
- universal indicator
- dropper
- straw.

Here is what you should do:

1. Add a little water to two clean test tubes.

2. Put one drop of universal indicator into one of the test tubes and observe its colour.

3. Place a straw into each test tube.

4. Ask a volunteer to gently breathe out a few breaths through the straw and into each test tube.

5. Is there a colour change in the indicator?

FIG 9.5

Carbon dioxide is a naturally occurring gas that is important for photosynthesis. It is produced during respiration, decay, fermentation, combustion and volcanic eruptions. Carbon dioxide is acidic and forms carbonic acid with water.

Check your understanding

1. What colour changes are observed when the following are added to an acid?

    a) Blue litmus paper
    b) Phenolphthalein
    c) Methyl orange.

2. Name three common acids.

Key terms

acid a type of chemical substance

indicators substances made from special dyes that change colour depending on whether an acid or alkali is present

Strength of an acid

We are learning how to:

- distinguish between substances that are acids and alkalis
- identify the strength of an acid.

Strength of an acid 〉〉

Activity 9.3

Exploring the strength of acids

Here is what you need:

- vinegar
- milk
- apple
- universal indicator solution
- small pieces of universal indicator paper
- tweezers
- spatulas
- scalpels
- experimental trays
- hydrochloric acid
- sulfuric acid
- nitric acid
- droppers.

SAFETY

Observe the safety icon on the acid bottles. All indicator papers should be held with the tweezers. Take care when using scalpels. Avoid spillage.

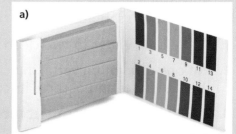
a)

Here is what you should do:

1. Copy the table. List the name of the substances you are going to test in the Specimen column, as shown below.

b)

c)

FIG 9.6 **a)** Universal indicator paper **b)** Universal indicator solution **c)** Experimental trays

Specimen	Universal indicator (colour change)	
	Paper	Solution
vinegar		
milk		
apple		
hydrochloric acid		
sulfuric acid		
nitric acid		

2. Using a scalpel, spatula or dropper, place a tiny sample of each specimen in the cavities of the experimental tray.

3. Wash your hands and all the apparatus you used thoroughly, and dry your hands.

4. Place one little piece of indicator paper in each specimen. Observe and record the colour change.

5. Add one drop of indicator to each specimen. Observe and record the colour change.

6. Were all the colours the same?

7. Do you think that the difference in colour has any significance for acid strength?

Universal indicator is very special. As well as indicating acidity, it also gives the strength of an acid.

FIG 9.7 As acidity weakens, the colour of universal indicator moves from red to yellow

Fun fact

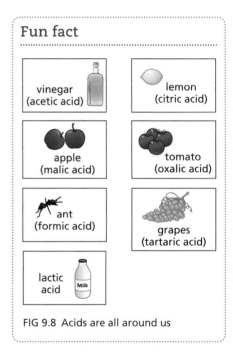

vinegar (acetic acid)

lemon (citric acid)

apple (malic acid)

tomato (oxalic acid)

ant (formic acid)

grapes (tartaric acid)

lactic acid

FIG 9.8 Acids are all around us

The colours of universal indicator match those on a range called the pH scale. Acids can have a **pH** with a number between 0 and 6. The stronger the acid, the more corrosive it is. The stomach produces hydrochloric acid, which is the strongest of all acids.

Check your understanding

1. How can you determine the strength of an acid?

2. Research what scientists use to make indicators.

3. Research what can be used to make homemade indicators.

Key term

pH measure of strength of an acid or alkali

Identifying alkalis

We are learning how to:

- distinguish between substances that are acids and alkalis
- give the colour change in an indicator when it is in contact with an alkali.

Identifying alkalis 〉〉

Activity 9.4

Exploring alkalis

Here is what you need:

- sodium hydroxide
- ammonium hydroxide
- calcium hydroxide
- blue litmus paper
- red litmus paper
- phenolphthalein
- methyl orange
- test tubes
- tweezers
- droppers.

 SAFETY

Observe the safety icon on the alkali bottles. All indicator papers should be held with the tweezers. Avoid spillage.

Here is what you should do:

1. Copy the table.

Alkali	Indicator	Colour change
sodium hydroxide (NaOH) ammonium hydroxide (NH$_4$OH) calcium hydroxide (Ca(OH)$_2$)	blue litmus paper	
sodium hydroxide ammonium hydroxide calcium hydroxide	red litmus paper	
sodium hydroxide ammonium hydroxide calcium hydroxide	phenolphthalein	
sodium hydroxide ammonium hydroxide calcium hydroxide	methyl orange	

2. Pour a few drops of sodium hydroxide into each of two test tubes.

3. Suck up a dropperful of sodium hydroxide from one of the test tubes.

4. Squeeze one drop of sodium hydroxide onto a piece of each of the coloured indicator papers and record the colour you observe.

5. Pour one drop of each of the liquid indicators into each of the two test tubes of sodium hydroxide. Record the colour change you observe.

6. Wash out all the test tubes and droppers thoroughly.

7. Repeat steps 2 to 6 for ammonium hydroxide and then for calcium hydroxide.

8. Compare the results you found for the various alkalis. Did all the alkalis give the same results for each indicator?

The word **alkali** is of Arabic origin, meaning dry. Alkalis belong to the set of bases but they are soluble in water, hence the name **hydroxide**. Dilute solutions of alkalis feel soapy and have a bitter taste. All alkalis conduct electricity. Alkalis can be identified by their colour changes with indicators.

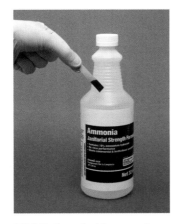

FIG 9.9 Household ammonia solution is strongly alkaline

Fun fact

Saliva is mildly alkaline. This helps to counteract the acids present in many foods.

Key terms

alkali a member of a group of substances that turn red litmus paper blue

hydroxide a compound of a metal with hydrogen and oxygen, which is often basic; if it is soluble it will form an alkaline solution

Check your understanding

1. Name three common alkalis.

2. What is the effect of an alkali on red litmus paper?

Strength of an alkali

We are learning how to:

- distinguish between substances that are acids and alkalis
- identify the strength of an alkali.

Strength of an alkali 〉〉

Activity 9.5

Exploring the strength of alkalis

Here is what you need:

- universal indicator solution
- small pieces of universal indicator paper
- tweezers
- spatulas
- scalpels
- experimental trays
- test tubes
- droppers
- bleach
- dishwashing liquid
- baking soda
- sodium hydroxide
- ammonium hydroxide
- calcium hydroxide.

 SAFETY

Observe the safety icon on the alkali bottles. All indicator papers should be held with the tweezers. Avoid spillage. Take care when using scalpels.

Here is what you should do:

1. Copy the table. List the names of the substances you are testing, as shown below.

| Specimen | Universal indicator (colour change) | |
	Paper	Solution
bleach		
dishwashing liquid		
baking soda		

2. Using a scalpel, spatula or dropper, place a tiny sample of each specimen in the cavities of the experimental tray.

3. Wash your hands and all the apparatus you used thoroughly, and dry your hands.

4. Place one little piece of indicator paper in each specimen. Observe and record the colour change.

5. Add one drop of indicator to each specimen. Observe and record the colour change.

6. Were all the colours the same?

7. Do you think that the difference in colour has any significance for an alkali's strength?

Universal indicator also shows the strength of alkalis. Universal indicator displays colours for alkalis with a pH between 8 and 14.

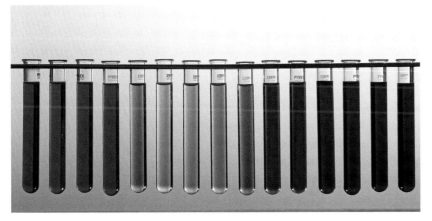

FIG 9.10 The colour moves from blue to dark purple as the alkali gets stronger

FIG 9.11 Alkalis are all around us

Alkalis can be found all around us, especially in the home.

So far you have identified acidic and alkaline substances. Based on the indicators, it can be seen that they are at opposite ends of the pH scale.

Check your understanding

1. What would the pH of a strong alkali be?

2. What numbers indicate the pH range of alkalis?

3. How does universal indicator show the strength of an acid?

4. Which number would indicate the strongest alkali?

Fun fact

An ant injects acid under your skin when it bites. By placing an ice cube on the bite, it is possible to soothe the sting and prevent swelling.

Acid–alkali reactions

We are learning how to:

- describe chemical reactions involving acids
- define neutralisation.

Acid–alkali reactions 〉〉〉

Activity 9.6

Exploring neutralisation

For this experiment you need to work in two groups: one with an acid and the other without.

Here is what you need:

- dilute acid
- dilute alkali
- liquid indicator (phenolphthalein)
- measuring cylinder
- droppers
- test tube
- straw.

 SAFETY

Observe the safety icon on the reagent bottles. Remember to observe safety rules when working with hazardous materials. Avoid spillage.

Here is what you should do:

Follow these instructions carefully and correctly.

1. Measure 1 cm³ of alkali and pour it into the test tube.

2. Use a dropper to place one drop of indicator into the alkali.

3. Observe and record the colour.

For the groups with the acid:

4. Using a second dropper, apply acid to the alkali in the test tube and shake it gently after each application.

5. Keep adding until a colour difference appears.

6. Use a third dropper to add drops of alkali to observe colour changes.

7. Add acid and alkali alternately until you think you have found a midpoint between acid and alkali.

8. Explain what you experienced as you changed from adding acid to alkali and back.

For the group with no acid:

9. Get one student to gently blow exhaled air through the straw into the alkali with the indicator.

10. They should keep exhaling until the colour changes.

11. Use the second dropper to add drops of alkali to observe colour changes.

12. Then the student should exhale into this combination.

13. Repeat until you think you have found a midpoint between exhaled air and alkali.

Alkalis are bases that are soluble in water. Acids and alkalis have opposite chemical properties. When an alkali and acid combine, there is a point where they both cancel out the effect of each other and this is called **neutralisation**. A neutral substance has a pH of 7, the midpoint of acids and alkalis.

Since acids and alkalis chemically react with each other, a new product is formed.

FIG 9.12 Carbon dioxide, which is slightly acidic, neutralises lime water, calcium hydroxide, which is an alkali

Key term

neutralisation the effect of acid and alkali cancelling each other out

Check your understanding

1. Describe how to explore the neutralisation of an acid by an alkali.

Neutralisation

We are learning how to:

- describe chemical reactions involving acids
- give the products of the neutralisation of sodium hydroxide and hydrochloric acid.

Neutralisation 〉〉〉

The components of a chemical change occur in fixed or given proportions. To know the exact amount of each chemical to be used for neutralisation, you can use an indicator.

Activity 9.7

Exploring neutralisation

This is a demonstration activity. You are to observe and record.

Here is what you need:

- dilute sodium hydroxide
- dilute hydrochloric acid
- conical flask
- methyl orange indicator
- titration apparatus
- evaporating dish
- Bunsen burner
- tripod
- gauze.

 SAFETY

Take care with chemicals and heat sources.

Here is what you should do:

1. Add one drop of indicator to 10 cm³ of sodium hydroxide, and mix in a conical flask.

2. Use the titration apparatus shown in Fig 9.13a) to find and record the amount of hydrochloric acid used for neutralising alkali.

3. Use the data to combine a fresh set without the indicator.

4. Pour some of the combination into an evaporating dish and place over a Bunsen flame.

5. As the liquid evaporates, reduce the heat to a gentle flame.

a)

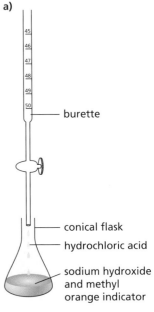

- burette
- conical flask
- hydrochloric acid
- sodium hydroxide and methyl orange indicator

FIG 9.13 **a)** Titration apparatus set up to find neutralisation point

b)

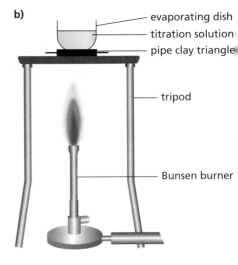

- evaporating dish
- titration solution
- pipe clay triangle
- tripod
- Bunsen burner

FIG 9.13 **b)** Evaporation of neutralisation

6. If it's a sunny day, some of the combination may be placed outside on a crystallisation dish.

7. When evaporation is complete, examine the residue.

8. Write a laboratory report on this activity.

c)
salt solution
crystallising dish

FIG 9.13 **c) Residue** from evaporation

The product of the neutralisation of sodium hydroxide and hydrochloric acid is a **salt** and water. The evaporation occurring was that of the water. The residue is the salt (sodium chloride). The chemical reaction that occurred is shown in this way:

sodium hydroxide + hydrochloric acid → sodium chloride + water

Was there any particular reason for the change to the gentle flame?

Check your understanding

1. What products are formed when a neutralisation reaction takes place?

Key terms

titration a technique in which the concentration of one solution is found by using another solution with a known concentration

residue the material remaining after distillation, evaporation, or filtration

salt the product of neutralisation

Products of neutralisation

We are learning how to:

- describe chemical reactions involving acids
- name salts from hydrochloric acid, nitric acid and sulfuric acid
- explain how a salt is named.

Products of neutralisation >>>

The products of the neutralisation of an alkali and an acid are a salt and water.

The names of salts have two parts. The first part is the name of the metal involved in the reaction. (Ammonia is not a metal but when it reacts with acid, the first part of the name of the salt is ammonium.)

The second part comes from the acid used.

If the acid is

- hydro**chlor**ic acid then the salt is a **chlor**ide

- **nitr**ic acid then the salt is a **nitr**ate

- **sulf**uric acid then the salt is a **sulf**ate.

FIG 9.14 The neutralisation reaction between ammonia (NH_3) and hydrochloric acid (HCl): the vapours from the stoppers combine to form the fumes of the product, ammonium chloride (NH_4Cl)

Activity 9.8

Naming salts

Name the salt produced from each of the following neutralisations:

1. The reaction of hydrochloric acid with

   a) copper hydroxide   **b)** zinc hydroxide

   c) lead hydroxide   **d)** magnesium hydroxide

2. The reaction of sulfuric acid with

   a) ammonium hydroxide   **b)** iron hydroxide

   c) sodium hydroxide   **d)** potassium hydroxide

3. The reaction of nitric acid with

   a) aluminium hydroxide   **b)** calcium hydroxide

   c) potassium hydroxide   **d)** ammonium hydroxide

Hydroxides are alkalis and are neutralised by acids. Here are some examples of the uses of hydroxides:

- aluminium hydroxide – antacids, deodorants
- calcium hydroxide – caustic lime, mortar, plaster
- sodium hydroxide – lye (for making soap), oven and drain cleaner
- magnesium hydroxide – laxatives, antacids

FIG 9.15 There are many different metal salts and some of them are brightly coloured

Check your understanding

Write the products of the following neutralisations:

1. magnesium hydroxide + hydrochloric acid
2. aluminium hydroxide + hydrochloric acid
3. copper hydroxide + hydrochloric acid
4. zinc hydroxide + hydrochloric acid
5. lead hydroxide + hydrochloric acid
6. aqueous ammonia + hydrochloric acid
7. aluminium hydroxide + nitric acid
8. sodium hydroxide + sulfuric acid
9. copper hydroxide + nitric acid
10. magnesium hydroxide + sulfuric acid

Fun fact

Although bee and wasp venoms carry a level of acidity or alkalinity, it is not practically possible to neutralise the venom because the insects deposit the venom under your skin!

Acid–oxide reactions

We are learning how to:

- describe chemical reactions involving acids
- give the product of an acid and oxide reaction.

Acid–oxide reactions ≫

Activity 9.9

What do you get when acids combine with an oxide?

Here is what you need:

- dilute hydrochloric acid
- sample of a metal oxide
- liquid indicator
- dropper
- glass rods
- beakers.

 SAFETY
Observe safety with chemicals.

Here is what you should do:

Follow the instructions carefully and correctly.

1. Scoop a little of the oxide and place it in the beaker.
2. Using the dropper, add one or two drops of indicator to the oxide.
3. What colour change did you observe? What does that tell you about the oxide?
4. Pour a little of the acid into the beaker and stir.
5. Pour a little more and stir until all the oxide dissolves.
6. Is there a change in the colour of the indicator? What does this tell you about the combination?
7. Add a little more oxide, and alternate between acid and oxide until you arrive at the neutralisation point.
8. Was there any fizzing? What does this imply?

An oxide is a base. If it is soluble in water, it forms an alkali. The pH of a base is between 8 and 14.

Most bases are **metal oxides**. This means that the positive ions are metallic and the negative ions are oxygen.

As with an alkali, when a base and an acid combine in the correct proportions, the chemical reaction – neutralisation – occurs.

As there was no fizzing, it indicates that no gas was produced.

When an acid neutralises an oxide, a salt and water are produced.

Check your understanding

Identify the products of the following neutralisations:

1. sodium oxide + sulfuric acid →
2. potassium oxide + nitric acid →
3. lead oxide + hydrochloric acid →
4. copper oxide + sulfuric acid →
5. zinc oxide + nitric acid →
6. magnesium oxide + nitric acid →
7. aqueous ammonia + sulfuric acid →
8. lead oxide + nitric acid →
9. iron oxide + nitric acid →
10. aluminium oxide + sulfuric acid →

FIG 9.16 Bases are used in the garden, kitchen and bathroom, as medicines and as laundry products

Fun fact

Copper oxide is used in many fungicides to protect crop plants from fungal diseases.

Key term

metal oxides substances where the positive ions are metallic and the negative ions are oxygen

Acid–carbonate reactions

We are learning how to:

- test the gas evolved from an acid–carbonate reaction
- describe what happens when acids react with carbonates.

Acid–carbonate reactions »

Activity 9.10

What gas is given off during an acid–carbonate reaction?

This is a demonstration lesson. Volunteers will be needed. Observe carefully.

Here is what you need:

- dilute hydrochloric acid
- samples of metal carbonates
- test tubes
- splint
- Bunsen burner
- limewater solution
- straw.

SAFETY

Observe care with acids.

Here is what you should do:

1. Place a little carbonate in a test tube.
2. Have a lighted splint available.
3. Pour some acid onto the carbonate and place the splint into the evolving gas. What happens to the flame?
4. Pour some colourless limewater solution $Ca(OH)_2$ into a test tube.
5. Allow the evolving gas to flow into the test tube of limewater and shake it.
6. What has happened to the limewater? Can you identify the gas?
7. Using the straw, exhale into a test tube of limewater. What do you observe?
8. What gas was exhaled?
9. Can you now identify the gas that was evolved from the acid–carbonate reaction?

When an acid reacts with a carbonate or a hydrogencarbonate, a gas is produced (evolved). To identify the gas, it must be tested. When a lighted splint was brought into the gas it was extinguished. When the gas was tested with limewater, a white precipitate resulted. Carbon dioxide is the only gas that forms a white precipitate with limewater. The gas evolved from an acid–carbonate reaction is, therefore, carbon dioxide.

Fun fact

In the 14th century, market traders used to try to sell chalk (a carbonate) as a hard cheese to innocent customers.

What else results from an acid–carbonate reaction?

Here is what you need:

- dilute hydrochloric acid
- samples of metal carbonates
- liquid indicator
- dropper
- glass rods
- beakers.

 SAFETY
Observe care with acids.

Here is what you should do:

Follow the instructions carefully and correctly.

1. Scoop a little of the carbonate and place it in the beaker.

2. Using the dropper, add one or two drops of indicator to the carbonate.

3. What does the colour change tell you about the carbonate?

4. Pour a little of the acid into the beaker and stir.

5. Pour a little more and stir until all the carbonate dissolves.

6. What does the colour change tell you about the combination?

7. Add carbonate and acid alternately until you are at the neutralisation point.

Carbonates and hydrogencarbonates are bases. Some bases are metal carbonates. When a carbonate reacts with an acid, neutralisation occurs as a new substance is formed.

FIG 9.17 Acid–carbonate reactions:
a) copper carbonate   **b)** sodium carbonate

Check your understanding

1. Describe the reaction between an acid and a carbonate.

2. What happens to an acid and an alkali when they react with each other?

Key term
....

carbonate substance containing a metal, carbon and oxygen

Completing acid–carbonate neutralisation equations

We are learning how to:

- describe chemical reactions involving acids
- give the products of an acid–carbonate reaction.

Completing acid–carbonate neutralisation equations ⟫⟫

Activity 9.12

Exploring the products of an acid–carbonate reaction

In this activity you will investigate what is left after CO_2 evolves.

 SAFETY

Take care with chemicals. Take care when using a heat source.

Here is what you need:

- hydrochloric acid
- sodium carbonate
- tripod and gauze
- evaporating dish
- Bunsen burner
- dropper
- beaker.

Here is what you should do:

1. Place some sodium carbonate in a beaker.
2. Carefully add some hydrochloric acid using a dropper.
3. Allow time for the reaction to take place.
4. Gently heat the reactants.
5. Place the product in an evaporating dish.
6. Use the evaporation method to discover the residue.

When an acid reacts with a carbonate, neutralisation occurs. The products of neutralisation are carbon dioxide, a salt and water. Just as in other neutralisations, the salt produced depends on the acid and the carbonate used.

carbonate + acid → salt + water + carbon dioxide

FIG 9.18 When calcium carbonate reacts with dilute hydrochloric acid, carbon dioxide is given off, which can be collected in a test tube

Check your understanding

Copy and complete the following reactions:

1. magnesium carbonate + sulfuric acid →
2. sodium carbonate + sulfuric acid →
3. copper carbonate + hydrochloric acid →
4. copper carbonate + sulfuric acid →
5. magnesium carbonate + hydrochloric acid →
6. ammonium carbonate + nitric acid →
7. sodium carbonate + hydrochloric acid →
8. copper carbonate + nitric acid →
9. zinc carbonate + sulfuric acid →
10. lead carbonate + hydrochloric acid →
11. ammonium carbonate + sulfuric acid →
12. potassium carbonate + nitric acid →
13. magnesium carbonate + nitric acid →
14. lead carbonate + sulfuric acid →

Fun fact

Carbonated drinks can become addictive in the same way as alcohol and other drugs. The body comes to want both the caffeine and the sugar hit provided by such drinks.

Acid–metal reactions

We are learning how to:

- describe chemical reactions involving acids
- identify the gas evolved from an acid–metal reaction.

Acid–metal reactions 〉〉

Activity 9.13

What happens when acids react with metals?

Here is what you need:

- rack of labelled test tubes, each containing a metal: aluminium, magnesium, copper, zinc, lead
- acid.

 SAFETY
Observe the name and the safety icon on the acid bottle.

Here is what you should do:

1. Take out each metal, observe it and replace it in the test tube.

2. Pour some acid onto each metal, shake gently, then feel the outside of the test tube. Look for any reaction and record any observations you make.

3. You can report your findings as a group. Did each metal react the same way to the different acids?

4. With which ones was there effervescence? What does effervescence indicate?

Metals react differently in dilute acids. Some metals show no reaction. However, when there is a reaction, effervescence occurs.

FIG 9.19 Reactions between metals and acids:
a) zinc and acid
b) magnesium and acid

To discover which gas is evolved during an acid–metal reaction

This is a demonstration lesson. You are to observe carefully.

Here is what you need:

- metal and acid that gave the best effervescence from Activity 9.13
- conical flask
- stopper
- Bunsen burner
- splint.

Here is what you should do:

1. Put the metal into a conical flask, add the acid carefully and put the stopper in to collect the gas.

2. Remove the stopper from the flask and bring a lighted splint over it.

3. What did you observe?

When a lighted splint comes into contact with hydrogen in the air, it produces a squeaky pop. This is because hydrogen is an explosive gas. Hydrogen is the only gas that reacts that way with a flame.

The gas evolved from the reaction of acids and metals is hydrogen.

When an acid reacts with a metal, neutralisation occurs. The products of this neutralisation are hydrogen and a salt. Unlike the other neutralisations, it is not possible for water to be produced because there are no available oxygen ions to bond with the hydrogen.

Check your understanding

Copy and complete these equations:

1. calcium + sulfuric acid →
2. lead + nitric acid →
3. aluminium + sulfuric acid →
4. zinc + hydrochloric acid →
5. magnesium + hydrochloric acid →
6. aluminium + nitric acid →
7. sodium + sulfuric acid →
8. copper + nitric acid →
9. zinc + sulfuric acid →
10. lead + hydrochloric acid →

Fun fact

Hydrogen is the least dense gas. In the past, hot air balloons were filled with hydrogen. However, because of the risk of explosions the use of hydrogen was discontinued and helium is now used to fill the balloons.

Formulae of acids and alkalis

What makes an acid? »»

Hydrochloric acid consists of a solution of the gas hydrogen chloride (HCl). Hydrogen chloride gas is a simple covalent compound but when it dissolves in water it forms ions.

$$HCl \text{ (gas)} \rightarrow H^+ + Cl^- \text{ (in aqueous solution)}$$

The important ion is the **hydrogen ion**, H^+. It is the presence of this ion in aqueous solution which is common to all acids. Here are the ions present in nitric acid and sulfuric acid.

$$HNO_3 \rightarrow H^+ + NO_3^- \qquad H_2SO_4 \rightarrow 2H^+ + SO_4^{2-}$$

When we use an indicator to test if a solution is acidic or not we are actually testing for the presence of hydrogen ions.

Hydrochloric acid, nitric acid and sulfuric acid are strong acids because they produce a high concentration of hydrogen ions in solution and turn universal indicator red.

Some acids produce much lower concentrations of hydrogen ions when in aqueous solution. These are called weak acids.

Vinegar contains a weak acid called ethanoic acid. Citrus fruit, like lemons, all contain a weak acid called citric acid.

Weak acids are much less dangerous and corrosive than strong acids. The food we eat contains a number of weak acids.

> **Fun fact**
>
> Sulfuric acid is described as a dibasic acid because it provides two hydrogen ions

Ethanoic acid   Citric acid   Tartaric acid

FIG 9.20 Sources of some weak acids

What makes an alkali?

The chemical opposite of an acid is a **base**. Bases which are soluble in water are called alkalis.

Sodium hydroxide is a common laboratory alkali. Here is what happens when we dissolve sodium hydroxide in water.

$$Na^+OH^- \text{ (solid)} \rightarrow Na^+ + OH^- \text{ (in aqueous solution)}$$

The important ion is the **hydroxide ion**, OH^-. It is the presence of this ion in aqueous solution which is common to all alkalis. Here are the ions present in potassium hydroxide.

$$KOH \rightarrow K^+ + OH^-$$

Sodium hydroxide and potassium hydroxide are strong alkalis. They produce high concentrations of hydroxide ions in solution and turn universal indicator purple.

As was the case with acids, there are some weak alkalis which still produce hydroxide ions in solution, but in much lower concentrations.

Ammonia is a gas which has the chemical formula NH_3. Here is what happens when it dissolves in water.

$$NH_3 + H_2O \rightarrow NH_4^+ + OH^-$$

Lime water, which we use to test for carbon dioxide gas, is a solution of calcium hydroxide, $Ca(OH)_2$.

$$Ca(OH)_2 \rightarrow Ca^{2+} + 2OH^-$$

Both of these substances produce low concentrations of hydroxide ions, OH^-.

ammonium hydroxide   calcium
(aqueous ammonia)   hydroxide

FIG 9.21 Sources of some weak alkalis

Activity 9.15

Identifying acids and alkalis in everyday life

You should work in a group of 3 or 4 for this activity.

There are a number of products we use every day that are acids or alkalis. Carry out research into products that contain acids and alkalis. Make a list in which, for each product, you give:

* its name
* whether it contains an acid or an alkali
* the formula of the acid or alkali if you can find it
* whether it is a strong or weak acid/alkali

Check your understanding

1. Here is what happens to aluminium ions when aluminium sulfate is dissolved in water.

$$[Al(H_2O)_6]^{3+} \rightarrow [Al(H_2O)_5OH]^{2+} + H^+$$

Would you expect a solution of aluminium sulfate to be acidic or alkaline? Explain your answer.

2. Here is what happens to carbonate ions when sodium carbonate is dissolved in water.

$$CO_3^{2-} + H_2O \rightarrow HCO_3^- + OH^-$$

Would you expect a solution of sodium carbonate to be acidic or alkaline? Explain your answer.

Key terms

hydrogen ion the ion formed by all acids in aqueous solution

base chemical opposite of an acid

alkali base that is soluble in water

Review of Acids and alkalis

- Acids are chemical substances that have a sour taste.

- Alkalis are chemical substances that conduct electricity and have a soapy feel when diluted.

- Both acids and alkalis are identified by the use of indicators made from special dyes.

- There are a variety of indicators used for identifying acidity or alkalinity.

- Universal indicator gives the degree of acidity or alkalinity using a range of colours numbered from 0 to 14.

- The midpoint on the universal indicator is green and indicates neutrality (pH 7).

- Carbon dioxide is a gas that can form a weak acid.

- Bases form a set of chemicals that include oxides, hydroxides and carbonates.

- Acids and bases can neutralise each other to form new products.

$$\text{acid} + \text{oxide} \rightarrow \text{salt} + \text{water}$$
$$\text{acid} + \text{hydroxide} \rightarrow \text{salt} + \text{water}$$
$$\text{acid} + \text{carbonate} \rightarrow \text{salt} + \text{water} + \text{carbon dioxide}$$

- Acids also react with metals to form neutral products.

$$\text{acid} + \text{metal} \rightarrow \text{salt} + \text{hydrogen}$$

- In order to identify a gas, it must be tested.

- CO_2 changes calcium hydroxide (limewater) to a white precipitate.

- H_2 explodes when placed near a flame, producing a squeaky pop.

- A salt is named after the reactants from which it was formed.

- Hydrochloric acid forms chlorides.

- Nitric acid forms nitrates.

- Sulfuric acid forms sulfates.

- Ammonia is a positive ion that takes part in chemical reactions.

- All acids release hydrogen ions, H^+, in aqueous solution.

- Alkalis are soluble bases.

- All alkalis release hydroxide ions, OH^-, in aqueous solution.

Review questions on Acids and alkalis

1. You have found a substance. Explain and give the results of three sets of tests you would carry out to discover whether the substance is acidic or alkaline.

2. Explain what you would do to determine how strong an acid or an alkali is.

3. When an acid neutralises a base, are the products acidic or alkaline?

4. Outline the steps you would follow to show that the result of neutralisation is a salt.

5. Complete the sentences by filling in the blanks below.

   Salts made from

   a) hydrochloric acid are _____.
   b) nitric acid are _____.
   c) sulfuric acid are _____.

6. During a reaction there is vigorous effervescence. Describe what you would do to conclude whether the gas evolved was carbon dioxide or hydrogen.

7. Show four different ways in which you can produce zinc nitrate.

8. Copy and complete the following chemical equations:

   a) zinc hydroxide + sulfuric acid $\rightarrow$
   b) magnesium carbonate + nitric acid $\rightarrow$
   c) aluminium hydroxide + sulfuric acid $\rightarrow$
   d) copper oxide + nitric acid $\rightarrow$
   e) lead + sulfuric acid $\rightarrow$
   f) sodium + hydrochloric acid $\rightarrow$
   g) aqueous ammonia + sulfuric acid $\rightarrow$
   h) potassium + nitric acid $\rightarrow$
   i) zinc carbonate + hydrochloric acid $\rightarrow$
   j) copper carbonate + nitric acid $\rightarrow$
   k) copper hydroxide + sulfuric acid $\rightarrow$
   l) lead hydroxide + nitric acid $\rightarrow$
   m) potassium carbonate + sulfuric acid $\rightarrow$
   n) magnesium + hydrochloric acid $\rightarrow$

Measuring soil acidity to improve yield

Mrs Whittaker's house has a small backyard garden in which she grows vegetables.

Mrs Whittaker grows vegetables with mixed success. She notices that some vegetables grow well while others do not but she doesn't know why. When she discussed this with another gardener in her community Mrs Whittaker was told that the pH of her soil was an important issue when deciding which vegetables to grow but she doesn't understand what this means.

You are Mrs Whittaker's nephews and nieces and she has turned to you for help.

FIG 9.22 Mrs Whittaker has a vegetable garden

1. You are going to work in a group of 3 or 4 to investigate soil pH. The tasks are:

   • to research about soil pH testing kits
   • to devise a method of measuring the pH of soil samples
   • to measure the pH of the soil in a garden
   • to research the best pH range for growing different vegetables and to recommend the best vegetables to plant in the garden
   • to research the use of lime to reduce the pH of soil and calculate the amount of lime needed to reduce the pH of the garden soil by a given amount.

a) Take a look at soil pH testing kits for sale in your local garden centre or on the Internet.

Each kit contains

   • **instruction booklet**
   • **pH colour chart**
   • **plastic mixing plate**
   • **plastic mixing rod**
   • **pH dye indicator liquid bottle**
   • **barium sulfate powder bottle.**

FIG 9.23 Soil pH test kit

Read the information on the box to see what they contain and how they work.

Use your knowledge of acid-alkali indicators and pH, and the information you obtain from the soil testing kits to devise a way of measuring the pH of soil.

Test the accuracy of your method by checking your results against those obtained with a pH meter.

b) You might investigate the soil in the garden of one group member or your teacher might divide up a plot of land and assign one part to each group.

Plan how you will measure the pH of the soil in the garden or given area of ground. You should consider such factors as:

- How many samples will you take?
- From which parts of the garden will you take your samples?
- How will you display your results?
- How will you use your results to provide an overall pH value for the soil in the garden?

c) The availability of different nutrients essential for plant growth depends on the pH of the soil.

For example, if the pH of soil falls below pH 6 plants find it very difficult to obtain phosphorus from the soil. Plants that need a lot of phosphorus will do badly in soil with a pH less than 6.

Research into which vegetables grow well in soils that have different pH values. Make a list of vegetables that grow best in acid soils. Make another list of vegetables that grow best in alkaline soils. Is there a range of pH values of soils in which all vegetables grow well?

Recommend which vegetables would be best suited to the soil in the garden.

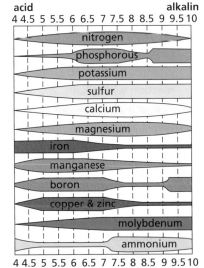

FIG 9.24 The wider the band the easier it is for the nutrient to be absorbed

d) Lime is a common name for several chemicals including calcium carbonate.

Investigate the effect of calcium carbonate on acids and explain the effect that adding calcium carbonate to soil has on its pH value.

e) Research how lime is used to reduce the pH of soil. Calculate how much lime per square metre would need to be added to the garden soil to reduce its pH value by 1 unit.

f) Give a PowerPoint presentation to the class on what you have found out about soil pH and the advice you will be able to pass on to Mrs Whittaker. Your presentation should include a demonstration of how you measure the pH of a sample of soil.

g) Plant some of the vegetables that you have recommended and cultivate them to see if they grow well. This will help you to determine whether your advice was accurate or not.

FIG 9.25 Raking lime into the soil

Index

Note: Page numbers followed by *f* or *t* represent figures or tables respectively.

Acknowledgements

pp6: crystal light/Shutterstock, pp6: Per-Anders Pettersson/Getty Images, pp9: Ian Miles-Flashpoint Pictures / Alamy Stock Photo, pp12: Geber86/E+/Getty Images, pp12: GLYN KIRK/AFP/Getty Images, pp13: SSPL/Getty Images, pp16–17: Christian/Darkin//Science Photo Library, pp16: Robert Fried/Alamy, pp17: MedicalRF.com/Getty Images, pp17: Dr G. Moscoso/Science Photo Library, pp17: Sebastian Kaulitzki/Science Photo Library/Corbis, pp17: Sebastian Kaulitzki/Science Photo Library/Corbis, pp24–25: BSIP/UIG/Getty Images, pp24: Kristoffer Tripplaar/ Alamy, pp24: Zoltan Kiraly/Shutterstock, pp25: Scott Camazine/Sue Trainor/Science Photo Library, pp26: Dr. David Phillips/Visuals Unlimited/Corbis, pp27: D. Phillips/Science Photo Library, pp28: Cavallini James/Bsip/Science Photo Library, pp28: Eric SA House – Carle/Getty Images, pp30: Stickney Design/Getty Images, pp30: Catherine Lane/iStockphoto, pp32: Science Photo Library – Mehau Kulykm Getty Images, pp34: Li Wa/Shutterstock, pp34: David Young-Wolff/Getty Images, pp35: Liba Taylor/Alamy, pp35: Wavebreakmedia/Shutterstock, pp37: Thony Belizaire/Staff/Getty Images, pp42–43: Gary Whitton/Shutterstock, pp42: Jamesbenet/Istockphoto, pp42: Michael Meshcheryakov/Shutterstock, pp44: A-plus image bank/Alamy, pp44: Joe Raedle/Staff/Getty Images, pp46: Harvey Meston/Staff/Getty Images, pp46: David Cumming/Eye Ubiquitous/Corbis, pp47: Caribbean Photo Archive/Alamy, pp47: Jaysunlp/Istockphoto, pp48: Dbimages/Alamy, pp48: Tigergallery/Shutterstock, pp48: Michael Macor/San Francisco Chronicle/San Francisco/Corbis, pp49: Raisman/Shutterstock, pp50: Family Business/Shutterstock, pp51: Erik de Castro/Reuters, pp52: Uk Crown Copyright Courtesy Of Fera/Science Photo Library, pp52: Kokkai Ng/Istockphoto, pp53: Visuals Unlimited, Inc./Science Stills/ARS/Getty Images, pp53: Amawasri/iStockphoto, pp53: Age fotostock/Alamy, pp54: FLPA/David Warren/Rex Features, pp54: Francesco De Marco/Shutterstock, pp55: Athens 2004/Alamy, pp56: Landrin Valérie/Alamy, pp56: Brent Davis/Shutterstock, pp57: Photoshot Holdings Ltd/Alamy, pp57: Planet Observer/UIG/Getty Images, pp58: Dr Keith Wheeler/Science Photo Library, pp58: Fredrik Forsberg/Alamy, pp58: Magdanatka/Shutterstock, pp58: M.H. Sharp/Science Photo Library, pp58: Dr. Morley Read/Science Photo Library, pp59: Dan Tautan/Shutterstock, pp59: Israel Hervas Bengochea/Shutterstock, pp59: Mike Cherim/Istockphoto, pp59: Derek Trask/Getty Images, pp60: FLPA/Rex Features, pp60: Miropa/iStockphoto, pp60: Kipling Brock/Shutterstock, pp61: Bob Wickham/Getty Images, pp62: Nouk/iStockphoto, pp62: Premraj K.P/Alamy, pp63: David Parsons/Istockphoto, pp66: David Nunuk/Science Photo Library, pp67: Kentoh/Shutterstock, pp67: Fabien Monteil/Shutterstock, pp69: arctic ice/Shutterstock, pp69: Jeff Greenberg/Alamy, pp69: Dburke/Alamy, pp70: hidesy/Shutterstock, pp70: Matka Wariatka/Shutterstock, pp71: Natalia Siverina/Shutterstock, pp72: Member/Shutterstock, pp73: Awe Inspiring Images/Shutterstock, pp73: Razvy/Shutterstock, pp73: Rob Byron/Shutterstock, pp74: Onair/Shutterstock, pp74: Douglas Orton/Spaces Images/Corbis, pp75: Rj Ierich/Shutterstock, pp82: Pulsar Images/Alamy Stock Photo, pp82: PJF Military Collection/Alamy Stock Photo, pp83: Rawdon Wyatt/Alamy Stock Photo, pp84–85: Kodda/Shutterstock, pp84: Indianstockimages/Shutterstock, pp84: George Tiedemann/GT Images/Corbis, pp85: Andrew Lambert Photography/Science Photo Library, pp85: Tarzhanova/Shutterstock, pp85: Sommai damrongpanich/Shutterstock, pp88: PhotoSerg/Shutterstock, pp88: PhotoSerg/Shutterstock, pp89: John Kasawa/Shutterstock, pp89: Krivoshein Igor Alexandrovich/Shutterstock, pp89: Sue yassin/Shutterstock, pp90: Volodymyr Krasyuk/Shutterstock, pp90: Paddington/Shutterstock, pp94: Sciencephotos/Alamy, pp94: Prasolov Alexei/Shutterstock, pp114–115: Africa Studio/Shutterstock, pp112: Thomas Holt/Shutterstock, pp112: AndjeiV/Shutterstock, pp113: Kelly Marjen/Shutterstock, pp113: Margo Harrison/Shutterstock, pp114: Sciencephotos/Alamy, pp115: BanksPhotos/iStockphoto, pp115: Matthew Cole/Shutterstock, pp115: Revers/Shutterstock, pp115: Andrea Paggiaro/Shutterstock, pp116: Phil Degginger/Alamy, pp117: Fedorov Oleksiy/Shutterstock, pp117: Peter Sobolev/Shutterstock, pp119: Terekhov igor/Shutterstock, pp121: Cordelia Molloy/Science Photo Library, pp125: Toshkaanvi/iStockphoto, pp125: Science & Society Picture Library/Getty Images, pp127: Gomolach/iStockphoto, pp129: Strelov/Shutterstock, pp136–137: Pakhnyushchy/Shutterstock, pp136: Elenamiv/Shutterstock, pp136: LatitudeStock – Ian Brierley/Getty Images, pp136: Juriah Mosin/Shutterstock, pp137: Zvezdica/iStockphoto, pp142: Lester Balajadia/Shutterstock, pp142: Karin Hildebrand Lau/Shutterstock, pp142: Goldnetz/Shutterstock, pp143: Norma Cornes/Shutterstock, pp143: Peter Mukherjee/iStockphoto, pp144: Idea Images/Getty Images, pp145: Katrina.Happy/Shutterstock, pp148: Lekcej/iStockphoto, pp149: Stocktrek Images/Getty Images, pp149: Teekid/iStockphoto, pp151: Worldswildlifewonders/Shutterstock, pp151: Thomas Nord/Shutterstock, pp152: Helene Rogers/Art Directors/Trip/Alamy, pp153: Bikeriderlondon/Shutterstock, pp155: Baevskiy Dmitry/Shutterstock, pp160: Andrew Koturanov/Shutterstock, pp161: Mikhail Varentsov/Shutterstock, pp168–169: Mr. High Sky/Shutterstock, pp168: Shahril KHMD/Shutterstock, pp168: Dwphotos/Shutterstock, pp168: Mikeledray/Shutterstock, pp169: Aaron Amat/Shutterstock, pp169: Modustollens/Shutterstock, pp175: PanicAttack/Shutterstock, pp177: Andrew Lambert Photography/Science Photo Library, pp186: ConstantinosZ/Shutterstock, pp190–191: R. Gino Santa Maria/Shutterstock, pp190: Svitlana-ua/Shutterstock, pp190: Gts/Shutterstock, pp191: Dr P. Marazzi/Science Photo Library, pp191: Stockphoto mania/Shutterstock, pp194: Coprid/Essentials collection/iStockphoto, pp194: Martyn F. Chillmaid/Science Photo Library, "pp194: Pulse/Fuse/Getty Images," pp195: Charles D. Winters/Science Photo Library, pp197: Giphotostock/Science Photo Library, pp199: Andrew Lambert Photography/Science Photo Library, pp204: Andrew Lambert Photography/Science Photo Library, pp205: Andrew Lambert Photography/Science Photo Library, pp209: Andrew Lambert Photography/Science Photo Library, pp209: Martyn F. Chillmaid/Science Photo Library, pp211: Andrew Lambert Photography/Science Photo Library, pp212: Charles D. Winters/Science Photo Library, pp212: Martyn F. Chillmaid/Science Photo Library, pp214: BlueRingMedia/Shutterstock, pp214: AlenKadr/Shutterstock, pp214: Roman Tiraspolsky/Shutterstock, pp215: MARTYN F. CHILLMAID/SCIENCE PHOTO LIBRARY, pp215: TREVOR CLIFFORD PHOTOGRAPHY/SCIENCE PHOTO LIBRARY, pp218: Ivonne Wierink/Shutterstock, pp218: R Ann Kautzky / Alamy Stock Photo, pp219: Koliadzynska Iryna/Shutterstock.